Scars

BENEATH
THE SKIN

Smith Paul

Dedication

To my amazing wife, Eloisa Paul, the woman of my dreams and proof on earth that God loves me:

Every word in this book is a piece of my soul that took courage to share with the world, and none of it would have been possible without her unwavering support and encouragement.

My wife has been my rock and my light in the darkest times. She held the fort as I worked on myself to become a man worthy of not only being her husband but also a good Christian.

Thank you for never judging me for my past, and instead becoming the savior I desperately needed.

Your undying love, loyalty, spirituality, and strong faith in my potential to overcome every trauma I have faced helped me become a better individual, a loving husband, and a devoted father to our four beautiful children.

Thank you, Eloisa, for helping me uncover a side of myself I never knew existed. I thank God every day for blessing me with a woman as resilient, faithful, and nurturing as you.

This book is dedicated to you, my love. It is a small token of appreciation for a lifetime of support you have given me.

About the Author

Coming from humble beginnings in Cap-Haïtien, Haiti, and immigrating alone to the United States at 15 years old to pursue higher education and establish several successful businesses, Smith Paul stands as an honorable example of an immigrant's American Dream.

Rising from poverty and abuse, he not only succeeded in bringing his entire family to the U.S. for a better life but also built his own family with a loving wife, four children, and two thriving businesses. In addition, through his service in the National Guard, he now feels it is time to shed light on the darker parts of growing up as a child of poverty and war.

Table of Contents

Dedication...i

About the Author ii

Chapter 1:The Sound of Silence 1

Chapter 2: When the World Was Still Small 8

Chapter 3: A Hunger Too Deep 17

Chapter 4: A Map of Hurt..24

Chapter 5: The Split Inside Me..32

Chapter 6: Learning to Forget...40

Chapter 7: Reclaiming the Body..49

Chapter 8: Returning to the Fire 58

Chapter 9: Naming the Wound 66

Chapter 10: Grieving What Was Stolen...............................76

Chapter 11: Letters to the Survivor & A Message to Every Part of You 84

Chapter 12: Naming the Wound, Breaking Silence, and Telling the Truth Out Loud 88

Chapter 13: Rewriting the Story 92

Chapter 14: Learning to Trust Again & Rebuilding Safety Inside and Out 99

Chapter 15: The Healing Toolkit 102

Chapter 16: Trusting Again To Navigate Love, Intimacy, and Friendship After Betrayal 111

Chapter 17: Rewriting the Story to Move From Victimhood to Meaning 118

Chapter 18: Letters to Survivors, You Are Not Alone 125

Chapter 19: The Healing Practice to Anchor Safety.........130

Epilogue: You Are the Evidence 142

Chapter 1: The Sound of Silence

"The Lord is close to the brokenhearted and saves those who are crushed in spirit."

— *Psalm 34:18 (NIV)*

Silence had its own sound.

It wasn't peaceful like the hush of dawn or the lull before sleep. But this silence was different; it was the kind that crackled. The type that buzzed in your ears when danger tiptoed through a room. It didn't ask questions, nor did it scream. It just... waited.

I grew up surrounded by that kind of silence.

Our home was a small concrete house on a broken street in Haiti. The kind of house you build little by little, paycheck by paycheck, and prayer by prayer. The walls were unpainted, the tin roof rusting at the corners, and the windows, when they had glass, were always half open to keep the heat from suffocating us.

We weren't poor in the romantic way, or as television showed. We were poor in the kind of way that gets into your bones. In a way where food was a question, and not a guarantee. Where "bathroom" meant an outhouse if you were lucky, and the water we bathed with came from buckets we carried on our heads.

My brother and I shared a thin mattress, and we would feel the floor. We learned early how to sleep still so we wouldn't wake each other, how to ration the bread so no one felt cheated. My mother was always working, selling goods in the market and running errands for people who had more than we did. I remember the strength in her arms, the stiffness in her back, the kindness in her eyes when she still managed to smile at us before collapsing into sleep.

But we never talked about what hurt, not really. In our home, emotions were swallowed.
Questions were dangerous, tears were useless, and secrets... well, secrets had a place.
They lived in silence.

The first time she touched me, I was too stunned to speak.

1

She wasn't a stranger. She wasn't someone my mother would have suspected. That made it worse; it felt like someone had stabbed me in my gut.

She was a girl who was seven or eight years older than me, and she used to live with us. I vividly remember how she walked through the front door with confidence, laughing with the adults. However, when no one was watching, he took what didn't belong to him.

My body froze, but my soul screamed.
And yet, I said nothing. Not because I didn't want to, but because I couldn't. *I simply couldn't.*

Afterward, I sat outside on the small cement step near our doorway and stared at the red dust that covered the street. I stared at the chickens scratched in the dirt beside me. I heard that somewhere down the road, someone was playing music, a soft and swaying konpa. I listened to the music with all my concentration until I realized that people moved and life went on. If someone was stopped, it was me.

In that moment, I understood what it meant to carry something alone. The silence wasn't just around me; it moved into me, and it stayed.

I was either five or six years old when I was first abused. There is one thing about abuse: it has a way of making time slippery.

From that day forward, the silence and I became companions.
I stopped asking for help.
I stopped crying in front of people.
I stopped looking adults in the eye.

The irony is that no one noticed, or maybe they did, and they didn't want to believe what that silence meant. Children in Haiti are taught from an early age how to behave. How to greet their elders with respect, how to stay quiet when adults speak, how to be helpful, clean, and polite. But what they don't teach us is what to do when our innocence is stolen. No one teaches us that we have the right to say no, and when the very people who should protect us are the ones who harm us, silence becomes more than a habit; it becomes a shield.

The Theology of Pain

I grew up believing in God, just like everyone else did. Faith wasn't optional; it was cultural.

God was present in our meals, in our greetings, in the way people shouted "Bondye beni ou!" as a kind of automatic punctuation when you'd sneeze. My mother prayed with a kind of conviction that made me think God must live right above our roof, and maybe He did. Which is what made my questions feel so dangerous. Because if God lived that close, why didn't He stop it? Why didn't He strike that woman/girl down? Why did He let me feel so alone?

I remember lying on my back on our shared mattress one night, staring at the ceiling with tears soaking into the thin fabric beneath me, and whispering into the dark:

"Bondye, ou pa wè sa?"
God, can't you see this?

No answer came.
The only thing I heard was silence. Again.

But this time, the silence didn't just belong to me; it felt like it belonged to God, too. Was I being punished? Was I bad? Was I unworthy of help? The theology I inherited told me that God rewards the faithful and punishes the wicked. So, if something terrible was happening to me, the conclusion was simple:

I Must Be Wicked.

That belief stayed buried for years. Even long after the abuse had stopped, I still walked around with the deep, unspoken belief that I had somehow deserved it. That my body had betrayed me. That God had seen, and He chose to turn away. He chose to turn a blind eye to my silent pleas, tears, and anger. It's a cruel kind of silence when you believe even Heaven won't speak to you.

The Mask I Learned to Wear

Outwardly, I was a quiet child who was respectful and neat.

I said "Yes, ma'am" and "Thank you, sir."

I kept my hands folded in church and never dared look adults in the eye too long.

People said I was well-mannered. A "good boy." But no one knew I was performing. It hurts me to say that survivors become excellent actors. We learn how to smile through nausea, how to laugh when our skin is crawling, how to sit still when we want to run. We learn how to shape-shift into whatever keeps us safest.

I wore my silence like a uniform.

Even at school, I never asked for help; instead, I tried to blend in behind my desk, stay small, and remain unnoticed. There was no space for boys like me, no language for what I was going through. Even if I had spoken up, I didn't have the words to name what had happened. In Creole, there were no child-friendly phrases for "I was violated." The closest terms were vulgar or too adult to understand. Hence, I had no option but to swallow the truth whole, and it sat inside me like a rock.

It made me avoid mirrors.
It made me flinch at praise.
It made me second-guess kindness.
Yet, I kept showing up.

The Day I Almost Told

There was one day I came close to screaming that *I HAVE BEEN THROUGH HELL.*

I was sitting with my cousin under the mango tree in the yard. We were peeling sugar cane and tossing the rinds into a pile. The light was soft, and that was the moment I felt safe.

And I don't know what prompted it, but I turned to her and said,

"Has anyone ever touched you… you know… in a bad way?"

She looked at me, blinked, and laughed.

"What kind of question is that? You watch too many foreign movies."

And just like that, the door was shut again.
I smiled, forced a laugh, and changed the subject.

But my heart sank.

The silence had won again.

What Poverty Hides and Exposes?

In Haiti, poverty isn't just a lack of money; it's a pressure cooker of silence. There were neighbors who knew something wasn't right, and you could see it in the way they watched.

You could feel it in how they chose their words. But speaking up could mean losing access to food, shelter, and stability. People knew, and they chose to stay silent, too.

We lived in a community where everyone struggled to make ends meet. Parents were overworked, underpaid, and often traumatized themselves. Children were expected to "be strong," to "grow up fast," to "stay quiet." So, what happened to me got tucked into the same pile as everything else: hunger, disease, abuse, grief. It was just one more silent thing we didn't speak of.

The only thing poverty taught us was how to endure pain and not how to heal it. The church, though full of prayer and fire, didn't always offer room for stories like mine.

There was deliverance for the drunk, for the adulterer, for the one with demons.

But for the child who had been touched? There was only vague talk of purity.

No space for grief. No scripture for shame. Or so I thought.

The Day I Heard My Pain Preached

One Sunday, a visiting preacher came. He was loud, animated, and full of passion. But near the end, his voice dropped. He leaned into the microphone and said, "There are people in here carrying things that were never theirs to carry. Things were done to them when they were too young to stop it. You are not to blame." The room shifted.

Something inside me cracked. Tears came suddenly, and I bowed my head so no one would see. I don't know if he meant me. But it was the first time I thought, maybe, just maybe, God did see and listen to my silent prayers or perhaps questions.

What I Know Now

Looking back, I don't blame the little boy who stayed quiet.
He wasn't weak.

He wasn't cowardly.
He was surviving.

Silence was his safety plan.
It kept him alive in a world that hadn't made room for his truth yet.

But silence doesn't heal.
It protects the wound but never treats it, and eventually, the wound starts to speak, through anxiety, through self-hatred, through depression, and through misplaced rage.

It took years before I could say the words out loud.
It took longer to believe that my voice mattered.
That healing was possible.
That God hadn't turned His face from me, He had been weeping with me all along.

Reflection Invitation

As we begin this journey together, I invite you to reflect gently on your own silence.

- Were there moments in your childhood that were never spoken of?

- What did silence mean in your household: protection, punishment, or survival?

- Can you remember a time when you almost spoke, but didn't?

- What would it look like to begin speaking now?

You don't have to answer aloud.
You don't have to share anything before you're ready.
But I want you to know,
Your silence protected you once.
But your voice can heal you.

And you are not alone anymore.

Prompt Reflection Page

Chapter 2: When the World Was Still Small

When the Body Remembers What the Mind Tries to Forget

"Do you not know that your bodies are temples of the Holy Spirit, who is in you…? You are not your own."

— 1 Corinthians 6:19 (NIV)

I used to think the abuse ended when the touching stopped. How naïve of me.

That once she left the room, once the door shut behind her, once the bruises faded, I was free.
But I didn't understand what trauma really does.
How it burrows.
How it memorizes.
How it teaches your body to flinch at shadows, even when there's no danger anymore.

I didn't know, as a boy, that my body would remember what I was trying so hard to forget.

It started with my stomach; there was a knot in it. It was something I couldn't quite name.

It was churning that never stopped, even when I hadn't eaten anything. I thought it was hunger at first, until I noticed it didn't go away, even when my belly was full. I'd feel it when someone stood too close behind me. I'd feel it walking past certain doorways. I'd feel it lying in bed, fully dressed, entirely safe, and yet I wasn't able to breathe.

No one teaches children about trauma.

They teach us how to pray, how to behave, and how to sit still in class.
But they don't teach us why our hearts race when there's no threat.
Why certain sounds feel like attacks.
Why does our skin go cold when someone touches our shoulder the wrong way?

That knowledge came later, when the damage had already etched itself into muscle memory.

The Day I Couldn't Breathe

I was maybe nine the first time I had what I now know was a panic attack.

Back then, it didn't have a name. All I knew was that my chest locked up, my vision blurred, and the air refused to enter my lungs, no matter how hard I tried to suck it in. I thought I was dying.

My aunt poured cold water on my face and slapped my back.
"Ou byen? Respire, ti gason!"
"Are you okay? Breathe, little boy!"

But how could I explain that it wasn't my body misbehaving, it was *remembering*?

A smell, a glance, or even a word was all it took.
One tiny thing, and suddenly I was back in the room.
Back in my small, shaking body.
Back in the silence.

Even though the woman was gone, my body was still reacting as if she were right there.
And no matter how much I wanted to forget, my body refused to.

Shame Lives in the Skin

I didn't understand the concept of "body-based trauma" until I was much older.
But long before I had the words, I had the symptoms.

I would scrub myself raw in the bath, trying to erase a sensation that never came from dirt.
I would avoid looking at my own body, even as a child, ashamed of something I couldn't define.

There were days I hated my skin, the shape of my body, and the fact that I had something someone wanted to take.

I carried that hate in my posture. I kept my head low, my shoulders tight, and my jaw clenched. I was always bracing, waiting. As if the next assault was a breath away.

Touch as a Trigger

It took me years to realize I didn't actually hate touch. I just didn't know how to trust it.

Every time someone hugged me too tightly, clapped a hand on my back, or even brushed against me in a crowded room, my muscles would tighten like a trap. I'd smile, nod, and play along, but my whole body was screaming.

Because back then, touch wasn't something that communicated love; it was something that announced danger.

Even safe people could feel unsafe if they moved too quickly or stood in the wrong place. Even loving gestures felt suspicious, and pleasure became confusing.

Trauma rewired my understanding of intimacy; it made me see it as a threat where others saw connection. Thus, my body reacted accordingly.

For so long, my body didn't belong to me.

The Lie of Overreaction

I was told more than once that I was "too sensitive."
That I needed to "man up."
That "what's in the past is in the past."

But trauma doesn't follow the clock, nor does it obey the calendar; instead, it shows up when it wants, and it shows up *in the body*.

That's the betrayal survivors often feel, we may not want to remember, but our bodies do. We may want to move forward, but our nervous systems pull us back.

You can bury a memory, but your skin remembers. Your heart remembers. Your breath, your fists, your shoulders, they remember too. Every inch of your body remembers the pain that you try to push somewhere at the back of your mind.

Therefore, what looks like an overreaction to others might actually be a **survival instinct** trying to protect you from pain that once felt unbearable.

The Body's Cry for Help

As I got older, my body began to protest in ways I couldn't ignore.

I'd get sick more often than others. Stomach pain, migraines, and muscle tension I couldn't stretch away. No doctor could find anything wrong. But deep down, I knew that my body was trying to speak what my mouth still wouldn't.

Sometimes I'd feel so exhausted I could barely move, even after sleeping ten hours. Other days I'd wake up shaking, with no memory of a bad dream, but every cell of my body pulsing with dread.

That's what trauma does when it goes untreated: it leaks to find the exits.

It shows up in autoimmune conditions, in chronic fatigue, in panic disorders, and in digestive issues. And for many of us, especially survivors who grew up in silence, it shows up as this confusing blend of physical suffering and emotional numbness.

We hurt, but we don't know why.
We ache, but we can't find language for it.

But our bodies do.
Our bodies *always* remember.

When I Finally Listened

It wasn't until I began learning about somatic healing, how trauma lives in the nervous system, that I realized I'd been gaslighting myself for years.

I wasn't broken.
I wasn't weak.
I was wounded.
And my body had been trying to keep me safe, the only way it knew how.

Through tight muscles, shallow breathing, fatigue, freeze, flight, and fight.

The miracle wasn't that I was still functioning.
The miracle was that I had survived.

Reclaiming My Temple

There came a day when I looked in the mirror and made a decision: *I want my body back.*

Not just physically, but also emotionally and spiritually.
I was tired of treating it like a battlefield, of apologizing for it, and of shrinking, hiding, bracing.

Scripture says that the body is a temple of the Holy Spirit, not a prison for shame.

That truth changed everything for me.

It meant I could begin treating myself with reverence.
It meant I could stop blaming my body for being violated.
It meant I could listen to what it was trying to say, instead of silencing it again.

Healing started with small steps:

- Taking deep, conscious breaths
- Placing my hand on my chest and saying, "You're safe now"
- Drinking water like it was sacred
- Sleeping when I was tired, not just when I had permission
- Letting someone hug me, and staying in the hug long enough to believe I deserved it

Bit by bit, I began rebuilding a relationship with the body I once disowned.

Dissociation: The Silent Exit

There were entire afternoons I couldn't remember.

Moments when I was "there" in body but not in spirit.

I'd blink and suddenly realize someone was talking to me, and I hadn't heard a word. My eyes would be open, but everything inside me had left the room.

No one explained that this was called **dissociation**.
I just thought I was weird, lazy, or broken.

But dissociation is one of the body's most protective responses to trauma.

When something is too overwhelming to process, the mind simply detaches.

You may still smile, function, and walk through the world.

But inside, you're far away, hidden in a safe corner where no one can reach you.

I remember once staring at a fan spinning overhead while someone argued across the room, the voices got louder, and the heat rose. I felt something in me float upward, as though I were watching it all from the ceiling.

There were no tears or movement; it was just silence.

I didn't know then that I was checking out because my nervous system had decided, *"This is too much. Let me protect you the only way I know how."*

And it did, over and over.

But that protection came at a cost: I began to lose trust in my own memory and questioned my sanity. The worst feeling was that I felt like I wasn't even real.

When Masculinity and Trauma Collide

Being a boy didn't shield me from trauma.
However, it did make it harder to discuss.

In the world I grew up in, masculinity meant strength, control, and stoicism.

You weren't supposed to cry.
You weren't supposed to freeze up.
You weren't supposed to be the victim.

And yet, I was all of those things.

The shame I felt wasn't just about the abuse.
It was about what the abuse "meant" in the eyes of others.
That I was weak.
That I had failed to defend myself.
That I was "less than" a man.

These weren't messages anyone said to my face.
But they were baked into the culture.

When I flinched at a hand on my shoulder, boys at school called me "sensitive."

When I refused to fight back, they called me soft.

And when I withdrew from touch altogether, they said I was "cold."

No one ever asked why.
No one ever considered that I might be carrying something too heavy to name.

So I internalized it.
I wore my silence like armor.
I tried to perform manhood while secretly trying to survive it.

And for a long time, I believed that healing wasn't even an option, because real men weren't supposed to need healing in the first place.

But that's the lie.

The truth is: **strength is not the absence of wounds.**
Strength is having the courage to face them.

Rewriting the Body's Story

Healing doesn't mean forgetting.
It means rewriting.

Our bodies once learned to associate touch with fear, voice with danger, and stillness with shame.
But they are not frozen in that story forever.
The body can learn a new language.
One built on safety. Dignity. Trust.

I started small.

I let myself feel joy in movement again. I began dancing alone in my room, not to perform but to reconnect.

I practiced lying still and breathing deeply, not because I was hiding, but because I was safe.

I also allowed gentle touch into my life from people I trusted, slowly, cautiously, with permission.

I even began to lay hands on myself in moments of prayer, not as punishment, but as a blessing. Placing my palm on my chest and whispering,

"You're still here. And you are good."

Reflection Invitation

If you are reading this and your body feels like a stranger...
If you're tired all the time, or anxious without knowing why...
If your skin flinches at kindness, or your breath shortens at the idea of rest, you are not crazy or broken. Instead, you are remembering, and your body is trying to help you heal.

You do not have to force it.
You do not have to hate it.
You can begin again, gently.

Here are some prompts to reflect on as you continue this chapter of your own story:

- What has your body remembered that your mind tried to forget?

- Are there physical symptoms you've been carrying without explanation?

- What messages were you taught about your body growing up?

- In what small ways can you begin to reclaim your body as your own?

- What would it look like to treat your body with reverence instead of resentment?

Prompt Reflection Page

Chapter 3: A Hunger Too Deep

Shadows in the Light: How Shame Taught Me to Hide in Plain Sight.

"People look at the outward appearance, but the Lord looks at the heart."

— 1 Samuel 16:7 (NIV)

I got really good at pretending. But it was not in the playful way that children imagine castles or slay invisible dragons, it was in the survivalist way, like how animals play dead when danger is near.

I learned how to make my face unreadable, my voice measured, and my presence quiet and agreeable.

If you met me then, you might've said I was "so polite" or "so well-behaved." You might've even called me strong, but you wouldn't know that it wasn't a strength; instead, it was a strategy.

One thing about shame is that it acts as a silent assassin, quietly seeping into your skin until you claim it as your own.

That is precisely what shame did to me. It began its slow, heavy descent into my body, and the only thing I knew to do was *hide*.

The Smile That Cost Me Everything

People always talk about the power of smiling, "Just smile and push through." "Put on a happy face." "Fake it till you make it." These are the most common teachings taught to children, but what about children like me? How do we make smile our friend?

For children like me, a smile was a mask; it was so tight that it nearly choked me.

I wore that smile to church, at school, and around the people who called themselves family.

Every time I put it on, I felt like I was abandoning myself, as underneath it, I was terrified, confused, and ashamed. I didn't feel like a whole person, more like a collection of pieces taped together to look acceptable.

The worst part was that no one could see what was underneath, and part of me was proud of that. I firmly believed that I had succeeded in becoming invisible, even when I was entirely in the room.

But another part of me that was a quieter, sacred part, was screaming: *"Somebody please see me."*

Two Selves, One Body

At some point, I became two people. There was the version of me that walked into church in pressed clothes, knew when to raise my hands during worship, and answered questions with a nod, a smile, a quiet "yes." Then there was the other me, the one who felt sick in his stomach when a woman stood too close, the one who couldn't sleep through the night without flinching, the one who carried a shame so deep it didn't even have a name.

I made sure to keep them separate.

I didn't know what dissociation was back then, but I lived it every day. I would float just above myself, watching my life unfold like a play I had memorized but never believed. Every word, every movement, was scripted to keep people comfortable, so they'd never think to ask the real questions.

This dual existence was exhausting, and it broke me a little more every day. Yet, it felt safer than telling the truth.

Shame Is a Shape-Shifter

The thing about shame is that it doesn't always announce itself clearly; like I said, it is a silent assassin. It doesn't always scream, "You are bad!" Sometimes it whispers, "Don't be a burden." "Don't draw attention." Or "Don't make people uncomfortable."

So, I learned to anticipate everyone's needs but my own, whether it meant that I offered jokes, silence, helpfulness, anything in between, but honesty.

Shame told me I was doing the right thing by disappearing inside myself. It rewarded me for being small, being agreeable, even for never crying too loud, needing too much, or making others feel awkward with my sadness.

Honestly, I believed everything shame told me, because when you're a child in pain, and no one reaches for you, shame becomes a kind of logic.

It is a survival manual written in invisible ink.

Performing Normal

I remember watching the other kids, and how easily they laughed, how freely they ran, how their bodies seemed light with play. I even tried to copy them, but I failed.

I made myself laugh when others laughed, even when I didn't understand the joke. I mimicked their walk, their slang, their carefree defiance. I built a version of myself that looked just enough like them to pass, but underneath, I was calculating every move.

Was that too much eye contact?
Did I react the right way when someone bumped into me?
Did I flinch when the pastor laid hands on my head?

I mastered becoming camouflaged.

Not because I wanted to deceive, but because I believed my true self was too damaged to be accepted. While people praised me for being quiet, respectful, and mature for my age, I felt the cost of that performance in my bones. Every compliment felt like a win for my mask, and every moment I "got away with it" felt like both relief and grief.

Spiritualized Shame

Church added another layer.

I was taught that the body was a temple, but mine felt desecrated. I was told that God was love, but I couldn't reconcile that with what had been done to me. I was encouraged to confess sin, but what was I supposed to confess when the sin wasn't mine?

Hence, I began to confuse abuse with guilt and to mistake trauma responses for spiritual failure.

I thought my triggers meant I lacked faith or my silence was disobedience. I viewed my trauma as something I had to repent for, not *recover from.*

So, I prayed harder.

I performed better.

I told God I was sorry for being "so broken," not realizing that He had never once asked me to apologize for surviving.

When Hiding Becomes Habit

There's a strange kind of grief that comes when you realize you've been hiding for so long, you don't know how to be seen.

Even when someone looked me in the eyes with gentleness, I didn't know what to do with it.

Even when a friend asked, "Are you okay?" I'd still say, "I'm fine," before I could stop myself.

By then, hiding wasn't just something I did, it was who I thought I was.

I didn't know how to be open without fearing judgment, how to feel without apologizing, or even how to trust the safety I longed for.

When you grow up with a secret this heavy, you become fluent in the language of concealment, you learn to smile with sadness still lodged in your chest, or to laugh even when your body is screaming for rest.

Eventually, you forget there was ever another way.

Unlearning the Disguise

My healing didn't start with a grand breakthrough. It began with a slow, terrifying decision:

What if I let someone see the real me, even just a glimpse?

The first time I did that, I trembled. But I shared a small piece of truth with someone I trusted. I expected them to turn away, pity me, and pull back; instead, they leaned in.

They didn't try to fix me; they didn't offer clichés. Instead, they just stayed. For me, that was the beginning of something holy: a crack in the mask and a shaft of light where I'd only ever known shadow.

It was enough to make me wonder: *What if I could live without the mask altogether?*

The Cost of Hiding

For years, I believed hiding protected me, and it perhaps did, for a while. But over time, it cost me things I didn't even realize I'd lost. Hiding cost me my authenticity, connection, and peace.

I struggled to form deep friendships because I didn't trust anyone with my truth. I couldn't receive love fully because part of me believed that if someone *really* knew me, they'd walk away. I couldn't relax in my own skin, because I had trained myself to stay tense and alert, just in case.

Hiding kept me safe, but it also kept me lonely. It gave me control, but it stole my freedom. It wasn't until I began to peek out from behind the mask that I realized the world was far less dangerous than the one I had built inside my head.

The Invitation to Be Known

Healing doesn't demand that we rip off our masks all at once.
It begins with **small, sacred risks.**

- Telling someone the truth when "I'm fine" feels easier.

- Letting your face show emotion, even if your voice still trembles.

- Choosing to stay present in your body when it wants to disappear.

- Trusting that even if someone rejects your truth, *you are still worthy of being seen.*

God never asked me to be perfect, He never called me to perform, nor did He call me to be real. In the honesty of that calling, I began to find something that shame could never offer: **belonging**, without condition.

Reflection Invitation

Shame wants to isolate you. It wants you to believe that your worth is tied to your ability to stay hidden, polished, and unbothered.

But God sees past all that. He sees the real you, and He does not flinch. You don't need to keep performing or keep hiding.

You are allowed to be *seen*, even in your sorrow.

You are allowed to be *known*, even in your fear.

You are allowed to be *held*, even in your healing.

Take time to reflect on these questions:

- In what areas of your life are you still hiding?
- What "mask" have you worn for so long that you've mistaken it for your identity?
- What would it feel like to be fully seen by someone safe?
- How do you believe God sees you, right now, exactly as you are?

Prompt Reflection Page

Chapter 4: A Map of Hurt

Foreign Tongues, Familiar Fears: When Identity Begins to Fragment.

"For here we do not have an enduring city, but we are looking for the city that is to come."

— Hebrews 13:14 (NIV)

I thought moving to America would save me. That once I left Haiti, left the street where it happened, the house where I couldn't sleep, the voices that didn't ask questions, I would finally be okay.

Unfortunately, I was wrong.

I misunderstood trauma. I forgot that trauma doesn't need a passport; it doesn't stay behind when you cross borders. It slips into your luggage, invisible and heavy, and hides in the folds of your accent, in the memories your new classmates can't pronounce.

I was no longer a boy from Haiti; instead, I was just a boy in America who didn't quite fit.

The Language of Loss

Creole began slipping from my tongue without permission.

At first, I still spoke it at home, whispering with my mother, issuing short commands to my brother, but even then, it felt like holding something that no longer wanted to be held.

Outside our house, I was desperate to belong. I started cutting Creole from my sentences like infected branches. First in school, then in church, and eventually in my thoughts.

Each word I let go of felt like a small betrayal, but it also felt like protection.

If I spoke like them, maybe they wouldn't see me as other, or maybe if I blended well enough, perhaps I'd forget what I had carried here. *I misunderstood again!*

But forgetting isn't healing, and belonging built on erasure isn't safety. Hence, I lost more than just words; I lost the part of me that remembered who I was before survival became performance.

Accent as a Warning Label

The first time someone mocked my accent, it didn't even make sense.

I hadn't said anything strange, and I'd answered a question, something ordinary. But the way my mouth shaped the words gave me away.

The kids laughed; their laughter was not mean, not malicious, just enough to let me know I was foreign.

In that moment, I understood something that would haunt me for years: the way I spoke marked me as different, and different was dangerous.

So, I began rehearsing how to sound "normal."
How to make my vowels stretch the way theirs did.
How to bite the harshness out of my consonants.
How to bury my tongue's memory.

I didn't want to be noticed; instead, I wanted to be invisible in plain sight.

Every time someone asked me where I was from, I'd pause before answering.
I wasn't ashamed of Haiti, not at all. I was afraid that their reaction would add one more layer to the mask I was already wearing.

I didn't have the words for it then, but now I do: that wasn't just self-consciousness, that was **survival**.

When Culture Becomes Costume

There's a difference between *being* Haitian and *performing* Americanness. Therefore, I learned early how to perform. I stopped wearing anything that reminded people of "home."

I downplayed the foods I liked, the music I recognized, the way my mom tied her headscarf at night. Even at church, I noticed how quickly people celebrated assimilation.

"You sound just like us now!"

"You're so Americanized already!"

They meant it as a compliment, but I felt like a ghost in my own skin.

Because every time someone applauded how well I blended in, it was a reminder of how much I had left behind to do so, and deep down, I feared I had traded authenticity for acceptance.

The Body Knows Before the Mind Understands

It wasn't just my language that changed. It was my posture, my pace, even the way I breathed.

I walked with smaller steps, spoke only when necessary, and, most importantly, avoided eye contact with people in authority, especially women.

It was like my body didn't trust the air, even though it was new air, streets, and walls, but the same old fear.

No one had touched me in months. I had moved, and I had a new life, but my body still acted like danger was right around the corner. It was because when you've spent years tensing for impact, you don't unlearn that overnight.

Hypervigilance became second nature. I scanned every room, read every tone, and I studied every woman's hands before he ever touched a doorknob.

Most people thought I was just quiet, but I wasn't silent; I was calculating, preparing, and bracing.

Even when nothing happened, it felt like something *could* happen. And that was enough to keep me on edge all the time.

An Internal Border Patrol

There were moments I questioned my own memory.

Was it really that bad?

Had I exaggerated it?

Why couldn't I just move on?

But my body never forgot, not when someone raised their voice, not when someone walked too close behind me, and not when I stood in a crowded hallway and suddenly couldn't breathe.

The past policed my present, and it guarded every doorway with the same question: *"Are you safe?"* And even when the answer was *yes*, my nervous system still said *no*.

The Invisible Grief of Identity Loss

No one tells you that grief doesn't always come with a funeral. Sometimes it comes with silence, with the quiet disappearance of things you used to love, or with the slow unraveling of who you thought you were.

I grieved in ways I didn't know how to name.

Grieved the foods that no longer tasted like home.

Grieved the holidays that didn't feel like a celebration.

Grieved the part of me that used to sing freely in Creole when I was little and unafraid.

I didn't tell anyone I was grieving, and I didn't think I had the right.

Because I had "escaped."
Because I was "blessed."
Because I was in America now.

But how do you hold gratitude and grief in the same hands? How do you thank God for a new beginning when your soul still mourns the cost of it?

I felt ungrateful for missing home and ashamed that even in a "better place," I still didn't feel safe.

Spiritual Displacement

Church was supposed to be home.
But even there, something felt off.

I didn't see myself in the sermons.
The worship songs didn't sound like the ones I grew up on.

And the prayers were always in English, never in the language my heart had first spoken to God.

I started to wonder if God had crossed the border with me.

Or if He was still waiting for me in the little sanctuary back home, where I used to kneel beside my mother's legs.

I tried to listen.
To believe.
To stay faithful.

But I felt lost in translation, spiritually and culturally, and I didn't know how to ask for help without sounding like I was complaining about a blessing.

So, I stayed quiet.
Smiled when asked how I was adjusting.
And nodded every time someone said, "God is good."

Because He is, but I wasn't.

Belonging by Disappearance

I became skilled at managing perception.

If I couldn't belong for who I truly was, I'd belong by **disappearing** the parts of me that didn't fit.

I laughed at jokes I didn't understand.
I nodded when I was lost in conversation.
I dressed like the other kids, even when the clothes didn't feel like mine.
I learned the slang. The codes. The ways of being that made other people comfortable.

Over time, I didn't just perform it, I began to believe it. I told myself I was "becoming" someone better; more American, modern, and Freer.

But it wasn't freedom, it was a quieter kind of bondage. The kind that feels like progress but tastes like forgetting.

Who Am I Without My Story?

One of the most challenging questions I've ever had to ask myself is: **Who am I if I can't tell the truth about where I've come from?**

If I erase the language that shaped me, the stories that raised me, the pain that marked me, what's left? I didn't have the vocabulary for trauma yet, but I didn't know that what I was doing had a name: **identity fragmentation.**

I just knew that I felt less and less like a whole person, and more like pieces I had to constantly rearrange depending on where I was and who I was with.

Eventually, at the core of that disconnection was the quiet, gnawing belief that my truth was too complicated to be welcomed.

Too foreign.
Too painful.
Too much.

Therefore, I continued the performance, hoping that if I perfected the mask, maybe someone would love me for what they saw.

Even if it wasn't really me.

Reflection Invitation

So many survivors live fragmented lives.

We smile in English and cry in our mother tongue.
We succeed on paper and suffer in private.
We move forward physically while emotionally frozen in the places we left behind.

But healing requires wholeness.

Not performance.
Not perfection.
Wholeness.

That means welcoming every part of your story.
Even the accents you tried to erase.
Even the griefs you were told to hide.
Even the culture you felt pressured to trade in for survival.

There is space in your healing for your **entire self**.
Not just the version others accept, but the version God has always seen, and never stopped loving.

Consider These Questions in Your Quiet Time:

- What parts of your identity did you learn to hide to feel safe or accepted?

- When did you first feel "too foreign" or "too different"?

- Are there cultural or spiritual roots you long to reconnect with?

- What might healing look like if it meant becoming *more* of who you are, not less?

Prompt Reflection Page

Chapter 5: The Split Inside Me

The Quiet Rage! How Anger Became a Language I Didn't Know I Spoke.

"Be angry and do not sin; do not let the sun go down on your anger."

— Ephesians 4:26 (ESV)

A Fire Without a Name

I didn't know I was angry, at least not at first.

I was well-versed with sadness, I was familiar with fear, and numbness was my best friend. But anger? That emotion had no place in the world I came from.

From where I come from, it wasn't safe to raise your voice, push back, and it definitely wasn't holy to feel that kind of fire.

What did I do? I swallowed it.

I told myself I was just "quiet." I told them that I had a calm personality and that I was more mature than my peers. But truth? I was just *trained* not to express rage.

Not when the abuse happened, when no one protected me, and when the world changed overnight, and no one asked how I felt about it.

The anger I felt back then did not go away. It just changed its shape. It settled in my jaw, always clenched, in my stomach, always tight, and lastly, in the way I snapped at little things or shut down when I didn't know how to express myself.

It showed up in my silence, withdrawal, and my deep need to control the things around me, so that I wouldn't break from the pressure inside.

That was my anger. It was just like silence; it did not speak, it wasn't noticed, yet it was always there.

The Lie of "Good Boys Don't Get Angry"

In church, anger was always cast as a sin. It was linked to violence, rebellion, and disobedience. They never presented it as a normal human response to violation; it was never treated as grief's loud sibling, nor was it viewed as a survival instinct demanding justice. Instead, it was called *sin*.

I learned early that good boys forgive and forget; they don't talk back, good boys stay composed, even when their world is burning.

So, I buried the rage deep inside and called it "peace," "godliness," and I even called it "healing." But repression isn't righteousness, it's just silence with a cross stitched over its mouth.

Where Does the Anger Go?

When anger has no voice, it doesn't disappear; it redirects. But my anger? It turned inward, giving rise to self-hatred, judgment, and perfectionism. I scolded myself for feeling too much.

I apologized for things that weren't my fault, and demanded excellence in every area of life because I thought if I could "get it all right," maybe the rage would stop echoing inside me.

But it didn't.

It only got louder, and quieter, too, in the way a storm gets quiet before it breaks. My body began to feel it long before my mind could admit it. I had stomach aches that wouldn't go away. Fatigue that sleep didn't fix. Muscles that stayed locked like I was bracing for an impact that never came.

That wasn't laziness.
It wasn't weakness.
It was unexpressed anger; compacted, internalized, and eating away at my peace.

Not All Anger Is Destructive

No one told me that not all anger is destructive and that some anger is *sacred*.

No one told me that God Himself gets angry, that injustice angers Him. Harm angers Him.

Oppression, silence, and abuse anger Him.

My anger was not rebellion; instead, it was proof that something inside me still knew what *shouldn't have happened*.

33

My anger was a cry for justice, it was a reaction to being treated as less than human, and a wound speaking in the only language it could.

And for the first time, I realized maybe my rage wasn't the enemy, and perhaps it was the evidence that I hadn't lost myself entirely.

Because the opposite of anger isn't peace, it's *apathy*.

And I was never apathetic.
I cared deeply.
I didn't know how to show it.

When Rage Becomes Silence

Some of the angriest people I've ever known never raised their voices.
They never hit walls, made threats, or yelled in public.

They just *shut down*.

Because silence can be just as loud, and withholding is its own form of fury.

I was one of them.

When I felt overwhelmed, I'd pull away. I never raised my voice when I was angry, I just disappeared. I never fought back; I just froze and stood there. The worst part was that I kept telling myself it was a matter of strength, and I was processing. When I was in reality, I was suffocating.

I didn't know how to tell people that I was in desperate need of help. How could I tell them, when I was taught to be "useful?" I didn't know how to tell them that I felt betrayed by the world and by God. But how could I tell them, when I was taught that good boys don't complain? I didn't know how to tell them that I had rage burning inside me like a furnace with no exhaust. But, again, how could I tell them that when I said that rage or anger is a sin?

So, I made myself smaller.
I turned my back on relationships when things got hard.
I avoided conflict not out of maturity, but out of fear.

Because I didn't trust myself to get angry without falling apart.

Making Room for Righteous Anger

I remember the first time I gave myself permission to feel angry and *not* feel guilty about it.

It was during a moment of prayer, actually.
Not soft or peaceful. It was raw, ugly, and loud.

I told God the truth: *That I hated what had been done to me.*

I was furious at the silence of those who should've protected me.

That I resented the pressure to be "okay" just because I survived.

And God didn't recoil.
He didn't chastise me.

I felt His presence settle like still water after a storm, not because the anger was gone, but because it had been *heard*.

In that moment, everything was changed.

I stopped seeing anger as failure.

I started seeing it as a flare, an invitation to tend to something I had ignored too long.

I didn't have to act on every feeling. But I did have to *listen*, because some truths won't surface until they're carried on the fire of rage.

The Cost of Repressed Emotion

There's a price to keeping everything inside.

For me, it looked like chronic tension, social isolation, and relationships that felt shallow or brittle. It was a persistent sense of not being known, even by the people who claimed to love me.

I didn't cry easily, but I also didn't laugh easily. I didn't explode, but I couldn't relax either.

I didn't break things, but I couldn't build anything lasting, because nothing real can be built on suppression.

And then came the shame.

Because when you repress anger, it doesn't just disappear. Instead, it mutates.

Sometimes into depression.
Sometimes into anxiety.
Often into self-sabotage.

I'd start fights with myself in my mind.
Pick apart every word I said in a conversation.
Rehearse imaginary arguments.
Live in fear of disappointing people, and then resent them for needing me at all.

That's the secret agony of the trauma survivor:
You are furious, but no one sees it.
And you are hurting, but you've gotten so good at hiding it that no one knows how to help.

Anger Is Not the End of You

For years, I was afraid that if I let myself feel angry, I'd lose control.
That I'd explode or hurt someone or never stop burning.

But healing taught me this:
Anger is not the end. It's the beginning.

It's the doorway to clarity.
It's the first sign that your soul knows something was wrong.
It's your body's way of calling for boundaries, for justice, for self-respect.

God gave us the ability to feel anger for a reason.
Jesus flipped tables.
David raged in the Psalms.
Even the prophets wept with fury at injustice.

Anger is not proof you're broken.
It's proof you still *care*.

And caring is where healing begins.

Learning to Speak the Language

I used to think healing meant no longer feeling angry.

That I'd know I was "better" when I could forgive without flinching and speak about my story without heat in my voice.

But healing doesn't mean *never feeling*.

It means feeling it **fully** and responding **wisely**.

I started to learn what my anger was trying to tell me:

- When I was irritated, maybe I had a boundary that was being crossed.

- When I felt resentful, maybe I was giving too much without replenishing.

- When I felt that old heat in my chest, maybe something sacred in me was crying out to be seen.

So I stopped shaming myself for it.

I stopped pretending I was calm when I wasn't.
I stopped smiling when I wanted to cry.
I stopped saying "it's fine" when it *wasn't fine at all*.

Instead, I journaled.
I prayed honestly.
I confided in safe people, people who could handle the full weight of my truth.

And little by little, my anger softened.

Not because it disappeared, but because it was finally *heard*.

When Anger Is Honored, It Transforms

Anger, like grief, is meant to move.

It's energy.
It's information.
It's power waiting to be channeled into something honest and redemptive.

When I started to honor it, anger became something sacred.
It taught me where I still needed healing.
It pointed me toward the child within me who still yearned for justice.
It reminded me that silence was never the solution.

And as I leaned into it, not recklessly, but reverently, I discovered something unexpected: **My anger was not the enemy, it was my ally.**

It was the part of me that refused to let pain go unnamed.
The part that wouldn't let me settle for false peace.
The part that still believed I deserved better.

Reflection Invitation

Anger is not a failure.
It's a flag.
It signals something sacred has been violated: your trust, your safety, your sense of being valued.

And for many survivors, it's the first honest emotion to return after years of numbness.

If you're angry, it doesn't mean you're bitter.
It means something in you still believes healing is possible, *or else you wouldn't care*.

Reflection Questions to Sit With:

- What were you taught about anger growing up? Was it allowed? Punished? Ignored?

- When you feel angry now, where do you notice it in your body?

- Who or what are you afraid will reject you if you express your whole truth?

- Can you remember a moment when you suppressed your anger out of fear of being "too much"?

- What would it look like to honor your anger rather than hide it?

Spiritual Anchor:

God is not afraid of your anger.

He can handle the storm of your honesty.
He *invites* it.

He is not a distant figure wagging His finger at your frustration. He is a Father who sits with you in the fire, unafraid of your heat, knowing it means you're alive and reaching for wholeness.

Prompt Reflection Page

Chapter 6: Learning to Forget

When Touch Betrays: Relearning Safety in a Body That Remembers.

"Do you not know that your bodies are temples of the Holy Spirit, who is in you…? You are not your own; you were bought at a price. Therefore, honor God with your bodies."

— 1 Corinthians 6:19–20 (NIV)

The Body Doesn't Lie

Long after I stopped talking about what happened, my body kept telling the story. It felt like my body was pleading for help, and it told me in different ways, it told me through flinches I couldn't control. It was told through the tension that lived in my shoulders like a second skin. I would also go numb during a hug, even a gentle one. It was told through how quickly I'd recoil from affection, even when I wanted it.

My body pleaded for attention and help, but I failed to understand it at first. I shrugged my thought, by saying, "Maybe I was just shy." Or "bad at intimacy." Or "overly sensitive."

But now I know better:
My body was doing exactly what it was designed to do: protect me.

My body remembered what my mind tried to forget, and it stored the terror in muscles, the panic in my chest, the silence in my skin.

Trauma lives in the body, and it doesn't just vanish when we move houses or change cities or try to smile our way through pain. Trauma leaves a strong imprint, and it lingers until you find the courage to face it.

Until then, it whispers, "Not safe," even when nothing obvious is wrong.

The Confusion of Good Touch After Bad

There were moments when I craved connection and moments when I yearned to be held, not just physically, but emotionally, and when I was offered that connection or moments, I turned them down, not because they were dangerous, but because I tensed. My body couldn't tell the difference between the good touch after enduring the bad.

For someone whose first experience of touch was wrapped in fear or betrayal, even kindness can feel threatening.

That's what trauma does: it rewires the alarm system.

It makes you suspect soothing, it makes love feel unsafe, and it even uses pleasure to trigger panic. But it does that because our bodies are meant to keep us from getting hurt again.

The betrayal wasn't just in the act; it was in the *confusion* of being touched in a way that was supposed to be gentle but wasn't. Being told "this is love" when it was actually violence.

Once you have experienced something horrifying, your body gets into survival mode, and that confusion sticks and runs deep.

Remember, your body takes time, perhaps a lot more than the time you anticipate, to unlearn that pain.

When Intimacy Feels Like Danger

There were times I wanted to run from love, not because I didn't want it, but because I didn't trust it.

That's one of trauma's cruelest tricks: It teaches you that the things you need most are the very things that might hurt you.

I would be in a room with someone who had pure intentions, and I would still feel trapped; I would still feel like someone was watching me, someone ruthless. I would place my palm on my chest and would feel my heartbeat speed up, my palms would begin to sweat, and my mind would scream, "Get out!".

The worst feeling is that I would know, the way my mind and body responded, it wasn't about *them*; instead, it was about what touch had once meant to me, what it had done to me.

For years, I didn't understand why I froze during intimacy.
Why I felt my spirit leave my body.
Why I felt ashamed after closeness, even in healthy, consensual moments.

Now I know: That was dissociation, it was a protective coping mechanism my nervous system developed during abuse. Even years later, that same system was still trying to protect me, even when I was safe.

Touch That Heals

For so long, I thought my body was the problem. I believed that I was too sensitive, confused, and broken.

But the truth is: my body was trying to save me.
It wasn't the enemy, it was the witness. The part of me that never lied, even when my voice couldn't speak.

Healing, then, wasn't about overriding my body.
It was about learning to **listen to it**.

To let it grieve.
To let it tremble.
To let it reclaim what was stolen, not all at once, but breath by breath.

Therefore, I made the decision to begin with small things, such as using a weighted blanket, a hand pressed over my heart in prayer, and wrapping myself in softness without rushing to "be okay." Eventually, with safe people, I let myself be held.

It took a lot of courage, time, and support from the people who cared about me.

At first, I braced for pain, but slowly, I discovered a new truth:

Not all touch wounds.
Some touch restores.
And not all hands hurt.
Some hands heal.

What the Church Didn't Say

In church, we were taught that our bodies were temples, but no one explained what to do when our temple had been invaded.

We were told to be pure, to wait, and to give ourselves to someone who loved us under God.

But what about when someone took before we could provide?

What about the shame that came, not from sinning, but from *being sinned against*?

There weren't sermons for that, nor did any one talked about the girl who couldn't make eye contact during worship, or the boy who sat stiff as stone when hands were laid in prayer, or even the teen who flinched at hugs and felt contaminated in their own skin.

So, we buried it and spiritualized our shame, calling it holiness.

We fasted to forget, served to silence the ache, lifted our hands while hiding our scars, and we wondered why healing didn't come.

God Sees What Was Done in the Dark

But God did not turn His face from what happened. He was not absent from the room, and He did not sanction the harm. He wept.

He bore witness when no one else did, and not with judgment but with deep, holy grief.

When Jesus touched the lepers, it was a scandal.
Because touch had been used to define who was clean and who wasn't, but He touched them anyway.

He crossed the line of shame and said, *"You are still worthy. You are still mine."*

I used to think God was disappointed in how I flinched, but now I believe He saw the flinch before it formed, and instead of demanding more, He offered stillness.

He never forced His presence on me.
He waited.
He stayed.

Hence, slowly, I came to believe that healing didn't mean pretending the past never happened: It meant inviting God into the places it did.

Reclaiming the Body as Sacred Ground

Healing didn't happen in a single moment.
It happened over hundreds of small ones.

Moments where I noticed my breath.
Where I stretched my limbs without shame.
Where I placed a hand on my belly and said, *"This is mine."*

There was a time I felt detached from my own body.
Like I lived beside it, not inside it.
It carried memories I didn't want, and feelings I didn't choose.

But slowly, I started returning, not forcefully, but because I began to understand: **My body is not the scene of a crime.**

It is the site of survival, it is the evidence that I lived, and in that light, even the parts I wanted to reject became holy ground.

Practices That Helped Me Come Home to Myself

I want to be honest, this wasn't just prayer and journaling.
This was **embodied** work.

Things that helped me include:

- **Grounding exercises** like placing my bare feet on the earth and reminding myself, *I'm here now. I'm safe now.*

- **Movement** without mirrors, dancing alone, stretching without critique

- **Gentle breathwork**, especially in moments of panic or disconnection

- **Loving touch**, even just wrapping my own arms around myself when no one else could

- Speaking out loud: *"My body belongs to me. And I choose to love it."*

None of these things erased the past; They reminded me that healing doesn't mean forgetting; it means **feeling differently** in the places I once felt afraid.

It means rewriting the story in my skin.
Giving it new meaning.
Letting safety become a practice, not just a hope.

Learning to Receive Safe Love

One of the most challenging things I had to relearn was how to receive *safe* love.

For years, I had lived in hypervigilance.
Always watching for signs of danger.

Constantly second-guessing the intentions of people who got too close.
Always wondering, *What do they really want from me?*

That fear was not paranoia; instead, it was pattern recognition.
A trauma-born wisdom that had protected me once, but was now keeping me from what I longed for most.

And healing began when I let myself test it.

When I let someone hug me and I didn't pull away, I just noticed how my body responded.

When I said, *"That touch doesn't feel safe,"* and didn't apologize for setting a boundary.

When I cried during moments of tenderness, not because I was hurt, but because I finally *wasn't.*

Sometimes, safety feels unfamiliar at first.
It feels too quiet.
Too kind.
Too gentle to be real.

But it *is* real.

And the more I leaned into it, the more I realized:
I could teach my body a new language.
One that spoke in calm heartbeats.
Open palms.
Unhurried affection.

God in the Flesh

Jesus didn't just come to save our souls.
He came in a body.

He touched the untouchable.
Was touched by the wounded.
Wept, bled, rested, and *felt*, just like us.

He understood the holiness of human flesh, and He honored it. When He healed, He often did it through **touch**.

Not forcefully.
Not without permission.
But with presence.

That tells me something sacred:
God still uses the body to restore what trauma tried to take.

Not only the body as metaphor, but *your* body.
My body.

The very body that once trembled in fear…
It can become a place of peace again.

Reflection Invitation

Touch is not just physical; it is emotional and spiritual.
It tells us who we are. If it's safe, it can say, *"You are cherished."*
But when it's weaponized, it confuses love with fear.

This confusion is not your fault.
It is a scar, a memory your body carries with wisdom.

But your body is not frozen in time. It can heal and learn again.

This process will not happen all at once and not by force, but gently, consistently, with love.

Reflection Questions to Sit With:

- What do you remember feeling in your body during moments of harm or fear?

- How do you respond to physical touch today, in friendships, relationships, even in prayer?

- Have you ever judged yourself for how your body reacts to intimacy or closeness?

- What would it look like to *bless* your body today, not just tolerate it?

- What small practice could help you feel more grounded and safer in your body?

Spiritual Anchor

Your body was never too much for God.

He knit it together.
He placed His breath in your lungs.
He called it a temple, *even now*.
Even after the tears, the shame, and after was touched without consent.

He still calls it good, and He isn't waiting for you to "fix" it; instead, He's offering to walk with you as you reclaim it.

Step by step, cell by cell, and memory by memory.

You are not just a soul with a body. You are a whole person, deserving of peace, belonging, and gentle love.

Prompt Reflection Page

Chapter 7: Reclaiming the Body

The Masks We Wear: Performing Wholeness While Quietly Falling Apart.

"Woe to you… You are like whitewashed tombs, which look beautiful on the outside but on the inside are full of the bones of the dead and everything unclean."

— Matthew 23:27 (NIV)

The Performance of Healing

There's a strange moment many survivors come to, when the outside begins to look "fine" again.

You smile in photos, show up to work, and volunteer.

You laugh at the right moments and give the right answers when people ask, *"How are you doing?"*

You've become a master of your mask.

But inside… something is still aching.

You lay in bed at night, staring at the ceiling, wondering, *if I'm doing so well, why do I still feel so hollow?*

This is the performance of healing; it's not fake, it's just **partial**. It's a version of you that learned how to function when breaking down wasn't an option.

High-Functioning Trauma

No one talks enough about **high-functioning trauma**.
The kind where you keep it all together so convincingly, even you start to believe the illusion.

You become the responsible one.
The dependable one.
The one who never complains.
The one who shows up early and stays late.
The one who's *"so strong."*

But strength, in this form, is often a cover for fear.

Fear of being seen as weak.
Fear of unraveling in front of others.
Fear that if you stop performing, no one will love the real you beneath the act.

I wore that mask for years.
It was the mask of the achiever, the good boy, the helper.
It looked like confidence, but underneath was a boy who didn't feel safe enough to fall apart.

Why We Learn to Pretend

Pretending isn't something we do because we're deceptive. We do it because we're **conditioned** to.

We learn early:

- If you cry, they ignore you.

- If you speak up, they punish you.

- If you show pain, they blame you.

So, we adapt, hide, and ultimately, *SURVIVE*.

We tell ourselves, *"If I'm just good enough, maybe I'll finally feel okay*, but performing doesn't heal the wound; it only covers it in glitter.

Healing won't begin until the mask cracks, just a little, enough to let the real light in.

When the Mask Becomes a Prison

At first, the mask feels like protection.

It helps you move through the world.
It keeps people from asking hard questions.
It lets you pass as "normal," even when you feel anything but.

But over time, that mask begins to weigh you down.
It becomes less of a shield and more of a prison.

Because no matter how many smiles you wear, no matter how many times people call you strong, you know deep inside: **They don't actually see me.**

They see the curated version, the polished version. The version that knows how to hold it all together without letting a single crack show, and being unseen in that way is a **devastating kind of loneliness.**

It's the kind of loneliness where people surround you, but still feel like no one truly knows you.
Like if they *really* saw you, messy, angry, grieving, confused, they might walk away.

So, you stay quiet.
You stay "fine."
You keep wearing the mask.

Breaking Free Without Falling Apart

But what if the mask isn't the only thing holding you together?

What if there's more strength in removing it and letting someone see the truth than in hiding behind it forever?

It doesn't have to happen all at once, and you don't need to take off the whole mask in front of everyone.

Start small.

- Let one trusted person see the fear behind your eyes.

- Admit, just once, that you're not okay.

- Let your journal hold the pieces you're not ready to say out loud.

These small moments of truth are what healing is made of.
Not big declarations, but *gentle honesty.*
Not performances, but presence.

And in those moments, the deepest miracle begins to unfold:

You are still loved, even when you stop pretending.

The Christian Pressure to Be "Okay"

Church was one of the hardest places to be real.

Not because God was unsafe, but because His people often didn't know what to do with grief that lingered.

They preferred praise reports to pain.
They wanted victory stories wrapped in bow-tied testimonies.
And I was still very much bleeding.

There's a pressure in some faith communities to be the *overcomer* before the overcoming has fully happened.
To act as if you've already forgiven, already healed, already moved on.

It creates this unspoken rule: **The longer you've known God, the less broken you're allowed to be.**

But trauma doesn't work on a schedule; it doesn't tidy itself up because you've been a Christian for ten years.

Whenever we attempt to "look heal" without actually healing, it only delays it, coming twice as painful as it was.

As we're so busy convincing everyone we're fine, we don't let ourselves bring our truth to God, or to people who can actually help.

God Is Not Impressed by Our Masks

Here's what I had to learn the hard way: **God isn't impressed by our pretending.**

He's not looking for the most composed version of us. He's looking for the *real* version, the one that still limps, the one that still cries out at night, the one that doubts, the one that rages.

And He doesn't turn away from that.

He leans in.

He touched lepers.
He wept with mourners.
He let a bleeding woman grasp His cloak.

Not once did He say, *"Come back when you've cleaned yourself up."*

So why do we say that to ourselves?

The mask might keep you accepted by people, but it keeps you **hidden from healing.**

And the longer you wear it, the more you risk forgetting who you really are underneath it all.

Why Vulnerability Feels So Risky

Taking off the mask isn't just difficult; it can feel *dangerous.*

Because for many of us, the first time we were vulnerable, we were hurt.

We shared our feelings and were mocked.
We said "no" and were ignored.
We asked for help and were shamed.
We opened our hearts and were betrayed.

So, the body remembers: *Vulnerability equals danger.*

That's not a weakness.
That's survival instinct.

But if we never risk being seen again, we stay trapped in a world where connection feels impossible.
And real healing only happens **in connection**.

That doesn't mean you bare your soul to everyone; it means you begin looking for people who feel safe enough to see behind the curtain, just a little at a time.

The Power of "Me Too"

One of the most powerful sentences in the world is:
"Me too."

It's the medicine that undoes shame.
The balm that says, *"You're not the only one who feels this way."*

But you can only hear "me too" if someone knows the truth of your story.

That's the paradox: We want to be seen, but we're terrified to show up.

Still, every time I dared to speak even a sliver of my pain to the right person, something shifted.

The mask loosened.
My chest unclenched.
And light began to pour into the places I thought would stay dark forever.

The goal isn't to live mask-free 100% of the time.
It's time to begin practicing honesty, even in small doses.

To ask yourself:

- "What part of me is tired of pretending?"

- "What would it look like to let someone see *that* part today?"

Because the longer you hide, the more healing you delay.

But every time you show up as you are, you reclaim a little more of yourself.

How the Mask Affects Our Relationships

When we perform wholeness, people relate to the version of us we present, not the version that actually needs love.

So even when they say kind things, we struggle to receive them. Because deep down, we know they're loving the *mask,* not the *mess.*

This creates a haunting emptiness:

- You feel praised, but misunderstood.

- Supported, but not truly seen.

- "Loved," but not fully known.

And that kind of love, while well-intentioned, can't reach the real wounds.

I learned that genuine intimacy requires honesty, and honesty requires taking a risk.

The risk of being misunderstood.
The risk of being rejected.
The risk of showing someone the mess and hoping they'll stay anyway.

And when someone *does* stay?
When they look at the unmasked version of you and say, *"I'm still here"*?

That's when something inside you begins to soften.
Because love that sees the truth and doesn't run, that's the kind that starts to heal.

The Invitation to Come Home to Yourself

The world might reward the mask.
But God does not require it.
Healing does not require it.

In fact, your healing will demand the opposite: that you come home to yourself.

That you learn to see the parts you've hidden with kindness.
That you begin to believe you don't need to earn love through perfection.
That you understand, *at your core*, you were never too broken to be seen and still chosen.

Removing the mask is not a weakness.
It is the bravest thing you'll ever do.

Because you are worth being loved as you are, not just as you perform.

Reflection Invitation

You've worn the mask for so long.
You've become fluent in its language.
You've played the role so convincingly that even you forgot it was a performance.

But now, the invitation is this:
To live without needing to perform at all.

To find a gentler rhythm.
To tell the truth, even in whispers.
To believe that you don't have to be "fine" to be worthy of love.

Reflection Questions for Gentle Honesty:

- What "mask" have you worn most often in your healing journey—perfection, strength, humor, spirituality?

- What feelings or truths might be hiding underneath that mask?

- When was the last time someone truly *saw* you? How did it feel?

- What would it mean to let someone see the real you today—even a small piece?

- What would it look like to love yourself without needing to appear strong?

Spiritual Anchor

Jesus didn't demand a polished version of you.
He never once said, *"Show me your strength, and then I'll heal you."*

Instead, He said:

"Come to me, all you who are weary and burdened, and I will give you rest."

— Matthew 11:28

He invites your weariness.
He welcomes your undone places.
He sees behind the mask—and still calls you beloved.

So if you're tired of pretending… if the performance is costing you your peace… you're allowed to stop.

You're allowed to rest.

You're allowed to be exactly who you are, right now, and still be met with mercy.

Prompt Reflection Page

Chapter 8: Returning to the Fire

All the Ways I Disappeared: Numbing, Splitting, and the Cost of Survival.

"He restores my soul. He leads me in paths of righteousness for His name's sake."

— Psalm 23:3 (ESV)

The Art of Disappearing Without Leaving

There are ways to vanish without ever leaving the room.

You can smile while your insides shut down.
You can nod and make eye contact while your spirit retreats to a quiet corner.
You can be the best-behaved child in the house while your body goes rigid and your mind floats far away.

This is the art of dissociation.
It's not drama.
It's not a weakness.
It's a life-saving brilliance our nervous systems create to keep us alive.

When the pain is too great to bear, the mind says, *let me carry you somewhere else.*

And so, we leave, not physically, but mentally, emotionally, spiritually.

We become ghosts in our own stories.

How I Learned to Split from Myself

I didn't have the language for it as a child; I only knew that certain things didn't feel real.
Certain moments didn't feel like they happened to *me*, and certain emotions felt like they belonged to someone else entirely.

Looking back, I realize now: I was disappearing to survive.

I learned how to stay quiet when I wanted to scream.
I learned how to laugh when I wanted to cry.
I learned how to become invisible when attention felt like danger.

These weren't personality quirks.
They were survival responses.

But over time, I forgot how to come back to myself.
I forgot how to *stay* in my body.
I forgot what it felt like to be fully present, unguarded, whole, here.

And while dissociation once saved me, eventually, it cost me: Intimacy, joy, and the chance to know who I really was.

The Safety of Numbness

Numbness is often mistaken for apathy.
But it isn't the absence of emotion.
It's the body saying, *"This is too much to feel right now."*

Numbness is protective; it dulls the ache when you have no language for the pain and helps you function when you feel like you're unraveling.

I didn't choose numbness; it chose me like a warm fog that rolled in when emotions became unbearable.

- When I wanted to cry, but didn't feel safe.

- When I wanted to scream, but no one would listen.

- When I wanted to disappear, and in some ways, I did.

Sometimes I envied people who could cry easily.
To me, tears felt dangerous. Vulnerable. Exposing.

So, I became stoic and controlled. Not because I was healed, but because I had learned how to freeze.

People-Pleasing and the Disappearing Self

There's a kind of survival that looks like being liked by everyone.

I became the helper, the pleaser, and the boy who said "yes" even when he was screaming "no" inside.

It felt safer to abandon myself than to risk disappointing others, and to mold myself into what people wanted than to assert who I really was.

This wasn't just a personality trait; it was trauma logic. Because somewhere along the line, I learned that pleasing others was a way to stay safe.

- If they were happy, maybe they wouldn't hurt me.

- If they liked me, maybe they wouldn't leave me.

- If I could just make myself easy, agreeable, invisible, maybe I'd be loved.

But every time I said "yes" when I meant "no," every time I laughed when I was hurting, every time I shrank to avoid conflict, a little more of me disappeared.

The hardest part? I didn't even notice I was vanishing, because the world rewards people who play small and call it "kindness."

Fawning: When Survival Looks Like Submission

You've likely heard of fight, flight, or freeze. But there's another trauma response: **fawning**, the act of appeasing others to avoid harm.

Fawning is:

- Apologizing for having needs

- Smiling to defuse tension

- Minimizing your pain to protect someone else's comfort

- Over-giving in relationships to feel secure

Fawning becomes a script: *If I can make myself likable enough, I'll be safe.*

It's not fake or manipulation. It's the nervous system trying to stay alive in an unpredictable world.

For children raised in unsafe environments, fawning can be a way to avoid emotional or physical punishment. But as adults, it robs us of boundaries, identity, and voice.

Because when you've spent your whole life shape-shifting to survive, you forget what your real shape even is.

The Fragmented Self

There were so many versions of me:

- The achiever who got straight A's

- The sweet church boy who never questioned authority

- The funny friend who always knew how to make others feel good

- The quiet one who swallowed his anger whole

None of them was fake; they were just **fragments**, pieces of me that had been separated to cope with different situations.

But I didn't know who lived underneath all those roles.
When someone asked, *"Who are you, really?"* I didn't have an answer.

Because trauma doesn't just wound the body.
It **splits** the self, and when that splitting goes unaddressed, you grow up feeling like a stranger in your own skin.

Like a patchwork quilt stitched together from other people's expectations.

When You Don't Know What You Want Anymore

One of trauma's cruelest effects is how it silences desire.

Not just romantic desire, but the desire to speak, to rest, to eat, to move freely, to be known, to be whole.

You spend so long catering to other people's needs that eventually, **you forget what your own even are.**

When someone asked what I wanted, I froze. Not because I was being polite, but because I didn't know how to access that part of myself anymore.

Desire felt selfish.
Choosing felt dangerous.
Voicing a preference felt like I was inviting disappointment or rejection.

So, I deferred and yielded.
I disappeared, one small choice at a time.

And I called it humility.
I called it obedience.
I called it maturity.

But really, it was just *absence*.

The Slow Return to Self

Healing doesn't require you to bulldoze your defenses.
It invites you to question them gently.

To ask:

- "What part of me am I still hiding?"

- "What did I once love before fear made me forget?"

- "Who was I before the world taught me to be small?"

This is not about becoming someone *new*.
It's about **coming home to who you always were** before the wounds.

And it happens slowly.

- The first time you speak about a boundary

- The first time you say "I don't know" and mean it

- The first time you notice what brings you joy without shame

Each moment is a thread that reconnects the pieces.
Each moment is a homecoming.

Because you were never too shattered to be made whole again.

Jesus, the One Who Sees Every Fragment

In the middle of my fragmentation, I often wondered:

Does anyone even notice the pieces I've lost?
Does God care about the girl I don't remember how to be?

And then I found Him, Jesus, moving tenderly toward the broken, the ashamed, the outcast.

Not commanding them to pull themselves together, but sitting with them in the dust.

He didn't demand wholeness first.
He offered belonging first.

He saw people others looked past, the bleeding man, the adulterous man, the unclean, the unlovable, and called them "son," "forgiven," "healed."

That's the kind of Savior who doesn't flinch when you hand Him your broken pieces.
He gathers them gently.
He names them worthy.
And He begins the slow, holy work of restoration.

The Beginning of Reintegration

To reintegrate doesn't mean forgetting what happened.
It means slowly reclaiming the parts of yourself that trauma told you to bury.

The boy who laughed loudly.
The child who dreamed freely.
The soul that danced without asking for permission.

Integration isn't instant. Sometimes it feels more like resurrection, slow, aching, miraculous.

You'll start to recognize yourself again.

- In your tears

- In your quiet "no"

- In your sudden craving for something you used to love

- In the stillness where God whispers, *"I'm making you whole."*

This isn't about perfection.
It's about **presence**.

Learning to live here.
In this body.
In this moment.
Without needing to disappear anymore.

Reflection Invitation

You may not remember when you began to disappear.
You may not remember how many pieces of yourself you've lost along the way.

But your body remembers.
And more importantly, God remembers the *wholeness* you were created for.

This chapter is not a call to rush.
It's an invitation to *notice.*

To gently observe the ways you've learned to survive.
To honor the brilliance of your coping.
And to begin, with kindness, calling the scattered pieces of yourself back home.

Reflection Questions:

- When did you first notice yourself "checking out" emotionally or mentally? What situations tend to trigger that response now?

- What role did people-pleasing or fawning play in your childhood? How do you see it showing up today?

- What desires, hobbies, or traits feel like "lost parts" of you?

- What would it mean to begin listening to those parts again?

- Where do you see Jesus in your story of fragmentation and return?

Spiritual Anchor

"He heals the brokenhearted and binds up their wounds."

— Psalm 147:3

You are not too fragmented.
You are not too far gone.
There is no part of you God does not see, and no version of you that is outside His reach.

Even if you don't know how to come home to yourself yet, He does. He will guide you there.

And every part of you, even the ones you left behind, matters to Him.

Prompt Reflection Page

Chapter 9: Naming the Wound

Naming the Wound: Breaking Silence, Telling the Truth Out Loud

"Have nothing to do with the fruitless deeds of darkness, but rather expose them."

— Ephesians 5:11 (NIV)

There is violence in silence.

It swells like a bruise under the skin. It is dark, hidden, and pulsing just beneath the surface. You carry it for years like it belongs to you, like it's a secret you were born to protect. But it does not belong to you. It never did.

Yet we, the wounded, learn to guard our pain as though it were treasure.
As children, we don't have the words.
As teens, we don't have the safety.
As adults, we don't have the certainty that our truth will be heard, let alone believed.

Thus, we say nothing.

But saying nothing is not the same as healing.
Silence does not make it disappear; it makes it fester.

I remember the first time I said the words out loud. It wasn't some brave moment of defiance. It was quiet, almost too quiet. It was a whisper into the dark, testing the air for danger.

My lips trembled before the sentence ever formed. I kept glancing over my shoulder, as if the walls themselves might turn against me.

Even though I was grown, even though I was far from Haiti, far from her, it felt like the moment I said it, the ground would break open beneath me and swallow me.

If I were to be honest, it did exactly the opposite of what I had thought. The ground didn't swallow me; instead, it set me free.

There's a kind of spiritual rot that grows in hidden places.

Abuse thrives in secrecy, and the enemy knows this. That's why darkness always demands your silence.

But God never told me to keep quiet. In fact, when I finally named the abuse, I felt His presence more clearly than ever.
It was as if He was saying, *"Thank you for trusting Me with this."*

He knew, He always knew. However, there is something powerful in *you* saying it, in giving the wound a name.

Because when you name it, you take it out of hiding.
When you name it, the shame loosens its grip.
When you name it, the wound becomes a doorway, not a dungeon.

But let's be honest, naming it is terrifying.

What if they don't believe me?
What if they think I'm lying, exaggerating, or confused?
What if I lose the little family I have left?
What if the abuser comes after me?

These are not irrational fears; they are the lived experiences of so many survivors.
Breaking the silence can cost you relationships, reputations, and entire identities built on false peace.

But the cost of silence is steeper.
Because silence costs *you.*

Naming the wound is a sacred act.

It is not for the world's consumption.
It does not have to be posted online or shouted from a stage.
Sometimes naming it looks like whispering it in a therapist's office.
Sometimes it looks like writing it in your journal for the first time.
Sometimes it's sitting in your car, gripping the steering wheel, and saying out loud, *"He and she raped me. They took advantage of my innocence."*

Each time you say it, it becomes less poisonous.
Each time you name it, you reclaim a piece of yourself.

There is no fear quite like the fear of not being believed.

It is more than embarrassment.
It is a visceral, suffocating kind of dread, the fear that your deepest truth might be dismissed as fiction, or your pain might be called a lie.

When survivors think about speaking up, we don't just imagine awkward silence or raised eyebrows.
We imagine outright betrayal.
We imagine someone we love turning their back.
We imagine being laughed at, called crazy, dramatic, unstable.

Unfortunately, for many of us, those fears aren't imagined; they've already lived through the misery.

I remember the first time I was doubted.

It was subtle, in a long pause, a slow blink, and a shift in tone.
They didn't call me a liar, but they also didn't lean in; instead, they changed the subject while looking uncomfortable. That was more than a hint for me to change the subject and suppress my pain.

Because for survivors, we are always scanning.
We are hyper-aware of people's reactions, we notice the breath they hold, the glance they avoid, the pity in their eyes.

It confirms the lie we were conditioned to believe:
"If I speak, I will be rejected."

Why does this fear run so deep?

Because, as children, we needed adults to protect us.
When they didn't, or worse, when they contributed to the harm, we internalized the idea that our truth is inconvenient, dangerous, or shameful.

When your abuser is someone others respect, admire, or love, you learn that truth becomes a threat to the illusion.

And sometimes, the illusion wins.

But silence is not the safer choice; it's the lonelier one.

Yes, speaking out may come at a cost.
But silence will cost you everything: your peace, your identity, your voice, your joy.

Even when others reject your truth, your healing is not dependent on their validation.

Your story is still true.
Your pain is still real.
And your healing does not require their permission.

God doesn't wait for people to believe you before He moves.

He believed you the whole time.
He saw the rooms you were in.
He heard the words, the silence, the sounds no one else was listening for.

> *"The Lord is near to the brokenhearted and saves those who are crushed in spirit."*
>
> *— (Psalm 34:18)*

He doesn't say, "I'll believe you if you cry hard enough."
He doesn't say, "Convince Me with your timeline."

He says, *"I saw. I know. I'm here."*

Healing begins when you start believing in yourself.

That's the first act of self-reclamation: trusting your own memory, your own knowing, your own gut.

Even if no one else claps for your story, even if your truth makes others uncomfortable, your courage will set things in motion; it already is.

Abuse doesn't end with the act itself; it echoes in silence.

The silence that follows is its own kind of torment, because what is left unsaid continues to grow in the shadows, until it distorts everything: your relationships, your identity, your God.

But when you speak, when you name what happened, you break the curse. The words become light in the room that held only shadows.

There is power in your voice.

There is spiritual power, psychological power, and generational power.

"Death and life are in the power of the tongue."

— (Proverbs 18:21)

And for too long, your tongue has been bound by fear. However, trauma loses its grip when we start to *talk back*. Not just to our abusers, sometimes not to them at all, but to the lies that abuse planted:

- *"It was your fault."*

- *"You wanted it."*

- *"You're dirty now."*

- *"No one will ever love you."*

Saying the truth out loud dismantles the narrative.

There's a reason evil always demands silence.

Because silence protects systems of abuse.
Because silence sustains shame.
Because silence keeps the cycle spinning from one generation to the next.

But your voice? It is a sword on that system's side.

When you speak, you don't just heal yourself, you cut a path for others.

It doesn't have to be loud to be powerful.

Naming the wound might sound like:

- "I was abused."

- "She touched me."

- "What she did wasn't normal."

- "That wasn't discipline, it was cruelty."

- "I was a child. They were an adult. That's all that matters."

Even whispered in a private space, those words rearrange the atmosphere. They become a declaration that you're not going to carry someone else's shame anymore.

Speaking your truth doesn't require an audience; it requires agreement.

Agreement with your soul, spirit who hovered over the chaos, and agreement with the God who is both Judge and Healer.

"Then you will know the truth, and the truth will set you free."

— (John 8:32)

Truth doesn't shame.
It shines.
It reveals what needs to be healed, not to hurt you further, but to make you whole.

Words unlock what was buried.

They carry grief, rage, lament, and even hope.
They are the tools by which we untangle the roots of our pain. When you name your wound, you open the door to name your healing, too.

There's a difference between exposing someone and healing yourself.

And for survivors, this difference can feel murky.
Do I speak because I need to be heard?
Or am I speaking because I want them to hurt the way I did?

This is where the waters of truth-telling can get cloudy.
The enemy would love to twist your healing into retaliation.
But God? He invites us into something holier.

You don't need to be pure to begin healing.

Let's say that first. You can be angry, messy, confused, and even vengeful, yet God draws near. He doesn't wait for your motives to be perfect and moves at the sound of your voice. But over time, as your heart starts to soften and your soul begins to untangle, you'll realize that **you don't need revenge, you need to let it all go and release yourself.**

There is power in confession, but not just for sin.

Confession, in the biblical sense, is about naming truth.
It is the practice of *agreement*, with what is real, with what is righteous, and with what is needed.

Therefore, when you speak the truth of your abuse, it is a kind of confession: "I am not the one who sinned." "I will no longer protect what was done in darkness." "I'm allowed to say what happened without apology."

This kind of confession doesn't expose itself to spectacle. It reveals for the sake of redemption.

You are not obligated to shame your abuser publicly.

Healing does not always require confrontation. Sometimes it does, but often, what's needed is **separation.**
Separation from the lies, from the role you were cast in, and from the silent loyalty that kept you bound.

Naming the wound doesn't mean dragging someone's name through the mud.
It means dragging the truth into the light where it can breathe.

Sometimes truth-telling is private.

A conversation with your spouse.
A session with your counselor.
A late-night prayer whispered to God while sitting on the bathroom floor.

Other times, it's a testimony shared with the intention of helping others.
But whatever the format, the *heart* behind it matters.

"Speak the truth in love."

— (Ephesians 4:15)

This doesn't mean speaking it softly.
It means speaking it with the intent to heal, not to destroy.

The goal is not to make them pay; the goal is to make you free.

That doesn't mean your abuser gets off the hook; justice matters as much as the truth matters. However, your healing isn't dependent on their punishment. Your healing is God's concern, and He takes it personally.

I was not a child anymore when I finally spoke.

But I felt like one. I felt five again, trembling, unsure if the words would come out right.
Unsure if I even had the right to say them.

I practiced first in my head, then in front of the mirror, on paper, and lastly, out loud.

I didn't tell my story to bring him down. I told it to bring *me* up.

I was suffocating in silence.
Carrying a secret that didn't belong to me.
And I realized, if I didn't speak, I would never fully breathe again.

There was no big audience, spotlight, or viral post. What mattered the most was that there were just a few trusted ears and just one voice, mine, but it changed everything.

The first time I spoke it aloud, it was like someone cracked open my ribcage and light poured in. The shame didn't disappear instantly. The pain didn't evaporate. But something else arrived in the room: **Power.**

There was no control or dominance, but the raw, trembling power of truth finally set free.

I didn't say it perfectly. You won't either.

That's not the goal.

The goal is not eloquence.
The goal is *liberation.*

Speak in broken phrases.
Speak in half-sentences if you must.
Speak with shaking hands, with tears, with long pauses.
You're not performing. You're healing.

Telling my story was the first act of reclaiming it.

It was no longer a horror I tiptoed around. It became a truth I stood beside.

Even if others didn't understand it. Even if they never said the words I wanted to hear. Even if they doubted or stayed silent themselves, *I* had spoken, and that was enough.

"Let the redeemed of the Lord tell their story."

— (Psalm 107:2)

Some of us are redeemed, but still mute. Still stuck between knowing the truth and daring to tell it.

But your story is holy, and when you name the wound, you also name the Healer.

Reflection Invitation:

- What would it look like to tell your story, not for justice, not for attention, but for liberation?

- What would you need in place to feel safe enough to speak?

- Who might be your first witness?

Prompt Reflection Page

Chapter 10: Grieving What Was Stolen

Grieving What Was Stolen: Lament, Rage, and Processing Loss.

"Blessed are those who mourn, for they shall be comforted."

— Matthew 5:4

Before I ever knew what had been taken from me, I knew I was hollow.

I was not empty, I was just missing something I couldn't name. It was a quiet grief; one I didn't recognize at first. I mistook it for personality or melancholy, and maturity beyond my years.

But in reality, it was mourning not for a person, but for a self I never got to become.

No one tells you how much you lose when you're abused.

Everyone talks about virginity, innocence, or boundaries.
But those are just the tip of the wreckage.

What about the safety of your own body?
What about the freedom to move through the world without hypervigilance?
What about your unshaped self, the one who could have bloomed naturally, instead of curling inward in defense?

Abuse doesn't just hurt. It *steals.*

And what it steals is layered, nuanced, lifelong.

I lost so many things I didn't know I was allowed to grieve:

- **My childhood rhythms** the way other kids played freely, without that edge of fear

- **My trust in adults,** not just the bad ones, but all of them

- **My voice** shriveled by secrets and survival

- **My ability to rest** was never guaranteed because safety was never guaranteed

- **My sense of being wanted**, I confused attention with affection for years

- **My faith,** at least the version of it that told me suffering was somehow my fault

Some of these losses weren't obvious until decades later. Some still surface in ways that catch me off guard, when I flinch at a gentle touch, or feel panic in a peaceful room.

Grief is not just for the dead. It's for the stolen.

For the stolen years. Stolen confidence. Stolen innocence.
Grief is the body's response to injustice.
It's how we honor what mattered, even if we never had it.

Jesus wept. He did not rush to resurrect without first joining the pain, and if God Himself paused to cry before healing, then surely our tears have a place too.

I used to think mourning made me weak.
Now I know it makes me *real*.
It makes me human. Whole. Holy, even.

There is a kind of worship in lament, a defiant kind of praise that says, "I am still here. And what happened to me matters."

You don't have to minimize the damage in order to move forward.
You don't have to explain away the ache.
You are allowed to grieve what was stolen, even if no one else ever named it.

I wasn't supposed to be angry.

Good boys don't rage.
They pray. They forgive. They keep the peace.

But deep inside me was a fire I could not deny.
And for a long time, I tried to suffocate it with scripture, with shame, with smiles.

It didn't work.

The fire kept burning.
Because beneath my grief was *rage*, and it was holy.

Anger, when denied, becomes depression.

It festers and turns inward.
Then, it begins to whisper things like:
"It's your fault."
"You should've stopped it."
"You're the one who ruined everything."

But when anger is *named*, it becomes power.

Jesus flipped tables.

He cracked whips in a holy place because justice had been mocked.
He didn't whisper when He saw exploitation, He shouted.

And still, we were taught to keep quiet.
To smile politely.
To be the bigger person.

But what if your anger is the *truest* part of you right now?
What if God is not offended by your rage, but standing inside it with you?

I was so afraid of being "bitter" that I almost never got to be *honest*.
But bitterness doesn't come from feeling too much; it comes from being forced to feel *nothing*.

My anger had a message:
"That wasn't okay."
"I didn't deserve that."
"You failed me."
"I will not carry your shame."

Those words needed a voice.
And rage was how they rose to the surface.

There is such a thing as righteous anger.

Anger that doesn't destroy, it purifies.
Anger that doesn't lash out tells the truth.

It took me a long time to learn that God isn't scared of my fury.
He understands it better than I do.

He burns with it too, not against me, but for me.

There were days I didn't want to cry; I wanted to *scream.*
And so I did.
Into pillows. In locked cars. In empty fields.
And I felt no shame about it.

Because healing is not always calm.
Sometimes it's thunder.
Sometimes it's storming the gates of your own silence and setting the record straight.

> ***"Be angry, and do not sin."***
>
> *— (Ephesians 4:26)*

This verse doesn't say *Don't* be angry.
It says: Let your anger come, but let it lead you to wholeness, not destruction.

You can rage without losing yourself.
You can rage and still be good, still be soft, still be beloved.

Your rage might be the sound of justice waking up in your bones.

Sometimes the deepest grief isn't for what happened, it's for what didn't.

The milestones were never reached.
The childhood untouched by fear.
The self you could've become if no one had broken you.

It's the ache of a life that was detoured before it even began.

This is called *disenfranchised grief,* a grief that isn't often named, because it's tied to what *could've been,* not what was clear.

But it's real, and it cuts deep.

I've wept for the little boy I might have been. He would have laughed more freely, trusted more quickly, and danced without needing permission. He would've loved without the shadow of shame clinging to his ribs.

But he didn't get to exist because someone else's sin interrupted his, and I mourn him like a funeral with no casket.

Abuse is not just a moment; it's a trajectory.

It shapes the way you see the world, bends your sense of normal, and rewrites your instincts and plants suspicion where joy should live.

Thus, when we grieve, we're not just mourning what happened.
We're mourning the personality we never got to grow into.
The relationships we sabotaged before they ever had a chance.
The ease we've never known.

This is sacred grief, and it deserves space, not shame.

There was a version of me that didn't flinch when touched.
A version that didn't over-apologize. A version that didn't second-guess his own voice, or brace for disappointment every time he smiled too long.

I don't know him, but I feel his absence, and I've come to honor him, too.

What helps me now is this:

I don't just grieve him, I fight for him.
Every time I use my voice, I do it in his honor.
Every time I set a boundary, take a deep breath, or let someone in, he rises up in me.

Maybe that alternate version of myself never fully got to be born.
But in healing, I become the next closest thing.

> *"He will restore the years the locusts have eaten."*
>
> *— (Joel 2:25)*

I used to think restoration meant getting everything back exactly how it should've been. Now I know it means becoming *whole*, even if the path was not what I wanted.

God doesn't give me the exact childhood I lost.
But He gives me something else:
A man who survived, a man who sees, and a man who now fathers the younger version of himself with power and tenderness.

The grief for what never was is holy, but don't rush past it, and don't silence it with toxic positivity.

Sit with it, bless it, and let it teach you what still matters to you, because grief reveals what we loved.

And love is never wasted.

Grief is not the end of healing; it's the beginning of depth.

It teaches you to slow down.
To honor what mattered.
To walk gently with yourself instead of rushing toward resolution.

At first, I thought grieving would drown me. But instead, it made me honest, and honesty set the stage for healing.

Grief clarifies what still matters.

When you finally let yourself cry for the little boy who didn't get held, you begin to hold yourself with more care. When you rage for the boundaries that were trampled, you begin to build stronger ones now.

You stop apologizing for needing space, shrinking to make others comfortable, and you stop pretending it didn't matter, because it did.

Grief, as painful as it is, becomes a kind of compass.
It points you toward what your soul still longs for.
Not to recreate the past, but to redeem what's left.

If you grieve the safety you never had, you'll begin to build a life where safety is sacred. If you grieve the trust that was betrayed, you'll begin to seek relationships that honor your vulnerability. If you grieve the voice you silenced, you'll find yourself speaking with more clarity and conviction.

The mourning becomes movement.

Not because you force it.
But because grief makes room.
Room for choice, for the agency, and for God to breathe on the ashes.

> *"To all who mourn... He will give a crown of beauty for ashes, a joyous blessing instead of mourning, festive praise instead of despair."*
>
> *— (Isaiah 61:3)*

This isn't about pretending the loss didn't happen. It's about letting the grief carve out space where beauty can grow again.

I found gifts in grief I never expected:

- A deeper empathy

- A clearer sense of justice

- A softness with people in pain

- A fierce awareness of what I will no longer tolerate

- A new closeness with God, not in spite of my mourning, but because of it

These are not consolation prizes.
They are treasures forged in the fire.

Grief doesn't hand you answers.
It hands you *presence*.
A way of sitting with your soul.
A way of tuning into the ache so that you can finally tend to it.

And sometimes, in the middle of all that ache, you'll find the beginnings of joy again, quiet, soft, but steady. Joy that doesn't cancel grief, but grows alongside it.

Reflection Invitation:

- What are you grieving, not just what happened, but what *never happened*?

- What losses do you need to name in order to honor your healing?

Prompt Reflection Page

Chapter 11: Letters to the Survivor & A Message to Every Part of You

"The Lord is close to the brokenhearted and saves those who are crushed in spirit."

— (Psalm 34:18)

To the You Who Doesn't Believe Healing Is Possible

Dear survivor,

I don't blame you for doubting.

When the pain has lasted longer than your memory, when the flashbacks show up like uninvited ghosts, when you've tried therapy, prayer, silence, screaming, and still you feel stuck, it makes sense that hope would feel dangerous.

Why believe in healing when surviving already feels like a miracle?

You've probably heard it before that healing is possible, that trauma doesn't define you, that God restores.

And maybe you nodded. Maybe you even believed it for someone else. But not for you. You've grown too used to the ache.

Too familiar with the numbing. Too tired to try one more method, one more book, one more "breakthrough."

So, you've learned to settle, cope, and make a decent home inside your pain.

Yet, *you're still reading.* Which tells me something: **There's a flicker in you that hasn't died.**

Healing is not a straight line.

It's not a staircase where every day is progress; it's more like waves, rising, falling, repeating.

Some days you'll feel like you're thriving, other days, brushing your teeth will feel like resistance against the dark.

This isn't failure.
It's *healing.*

He heals the brokenhearted and binds up their wounds.

— (Psalm 147:3)

God doesn't heal you like a mechanic fixes a car. He heals like a gardener, slowly, tenderly, with seasons.

He doesn't expect you to sprint toward wholeness; instead, He invites you to *rest* in it.

Maybe you're still confused about being triggered and not being healed. Maybe you've measured your progress by how *normal* you feel, but healing is less about erasing pain and more about expanding your capacity for life, love, and truth, despite the pain.

It's the ability to sit with your story and not dissolve.
To feel sadness without drowning.
To feel anger without shame.
To feel joy without fear.

Even doubting your healing *is part of healing.*

You don't have to fake belief to make progress, nor do you have to be perfect to be worthy of peace.

You just have to stay in the room with yourself.

Even when you're unsure.
Even when your hands shake.
Even when you want to run.

That's what courage looks like here.

God is not in a hurry; He's not measuring your faith by how fast you "get over it", He's measuring by how honestly you bring your wounds to Him, and He never once recoils.

So no, healing may not look like what you imagined; it might not come all at once, but it will come.

Not just because you're trying hard, but because God is *relentlessly* committed to your restoration.

You will not be in pieces forever.

Reflection Invitation:

- Which parts of you feel most distant or disconnected right now?

- How might you begin creating safety for them to return?

Prompt Reflection Page

Chapter 12: Naming the Wound, Breaking Silence, and Telling the Truth Out Loud

The Courage to Be Believed: Telling Your Story in a World That Isn't Always Safe

There is a unique terror in telling your story out loud for the first time: **What if they don't believe me?**

That question has silenced more survivors than any threat ever could.

Because when the world doubts your truth, it doesn't just feel like rejection. It feels like *reliving the abuse.*

You already lost your voice once; you were silenced, dismissed, and erased. Hence, when you finally gather the strength to speak,
You are not just telling your story, you are reclaiming your soul.

Therefore, if someone questions it, laughs at it, shrinks from it,
it feels like being violated all over again.

That fear is valid, but so is your truth.

You are not responsible for someone else's comfort. You are not required to present your trauma in a way that makes it easy to digest. You don't have to soften the edges or skip the ugly parts. You are allowed to tell your story in its *rawest, truest* form.

And here's what's even harder: Not everyone deserves your story, and not everyone is safe enough to hold it.

But that doesn't make it any less *true.*

The light shines in the darkness, and the darkness has not overcome it.

— (John 1:5)

Your truth is light, and no amount of disbelief can put it out. You may have already tried to tell someone, a parent, a friend, or a pastor, and they didn't listen.
Or worse, they blamed you.

Or changed the subject.
Or acted like you were exaggerating.

That's not just hurtful, it's *traumatizing*.

If that happened to you, I'm so sorry; that was not your fault either.
You were brave, and you *still are*.

You don't need external validation to confirm what you already know deep inside.
Your story is real.
Your memory is valid.
Your voice is powerful.

Even if they can't hear it, God does.

There are safe people out there, such as therapists, support groups, and survivor communities, who will *not* flinch when you speak, *not* rush you, and will hold space with reverence and care.

Find them and tell your story where it will be honored, not questioned.

And if you're not ready to share out loud yet, that's okay, too.
Writing it down.
Saying it in prayer.
Speak it to yourself in the mirror.
These are also sacred acts of truth-telling.

You do not need to be believed by everyone.

You only need to believe in *yourself.*

Because every time you say, "It happened," you are stitching together the torn places of your own heart.

And every time you whisper, "It wasn't my fault," You're speaking freedom into the parts of you that still feel trapped.

You are not invisible.
You are not delusional.
You are not alone.

Reflection Invitation:

- Where in your healing have you avoided grief out of fear that it might overwhelm you?

- What would it look like to give yourself permission to mourn, even in a small way, this week?

Prompt Reflection Page

Chapter 13: Rewriting the Story

Part I: The Ache for Justice

The Unseen Funeral: What Abuse Took Without Asking.

"He heals the brokenhearted and binds up their wounds."

— Psalm 147:3

There are funerals we never get to attend. Black dresses that we don't wear, flowers that we do not leave at our loved one's grave. This is what happens when you ache: there is just a quiet knowing that something sacred died, and no one noticed but us.

That's what childhood sexual abuse does: it steals things too intangible to name in a police report, yet they are too sacred to explain in a courtroom.

It took your innocence, long before you understood what innocence meant. It took your trust, especially in those who were supposed to protect you.

It took your sense of safety, your natural right to exist freely in your body, and your ability to fall asleep without scanning for danger.

And worst of all? It often took it all *without anyone noticing.*

You do not have any funerals, mourning, or even moments of collective grief. It is just you who is carrying the coffin of your childhood in secret.

There's a grief that survivors carry that the world doesn't see. It's not just about the events that happened; it's about everything that *should* have happened but didn't.

You should have had parents who noticed, teachers who asked questions, and community members who intervened.

You should have *believed*, and you should have been *safe*.

That grief is valid, and it doesn't mean you're stuck. It means you're human.

To grieve what was stolen is not a sign of weakness.

It's sacred honesty.

> *He heals the brokenhearted and binds up their wounds.*
>
> *— (Psalm 147:3)*

God doesn't rush your grief.
He doesn't say "move on."
He sits with you in it.

He was there when the taking happened. He saw it all, and now He longs to walk you through the mourning process, not around it.

You may not even realize how much was taken until years later.
When you struggle to trust your spouse.
When your body flinches from intimacy.
When you feel rage toward a child's innocence, because yours was never protected.

That's grief, too.

Not dramatic.
Not overblown.
Just real.

You are allowed to name what you lost, even if it feels invisible, and if it sounds strange to someone who hasn't lived it, because naming the loss is the first step to *honoring it.*

You're not being ungrateful, too sensitive, or holding a mirror to your soul and saying: "I see you. And what happened to you *matters.*"

You may never get the apology you deserve.
You may never see justice in the ways you hoped.
But this, this space to grieve, is justice of another kind.

It's the reclaiming of your right to feel.
To mourn.
To say, "Something was taken from me, and it wasn't okay."

Part II: Letting Lament Speak

Somewhere along the way, many of us were taught that being "strong" meant staying quiet.
That real faith was calm, that healing was neat, and that grief should be hidden in polite prayers and whispered pain. But that's not what Scripture teaches, and that's not how healing works.

Lament is not rebellion; it's a sacred language.

The Bible is full of lament:
David tore his clothes and wailed.
Jeremiah cried out in anguish.
Jesus Himself wept until He bled.

Lament isn't a breakdown in faith.
It's a *deep expression* of it.

It says:

"I believe God can handle my truth."

"I believe He won't leave when I scream or sob or shake with rage."

"I believe my cries matter to the One who formed my lungs."

"My God, my God, why have you forsaken me?"

— (Matthew 27:46)

Even Jesus spoke the language of sorrow, and He was not rebuked for it. He was *seen.*

When you cry out, you are not falling apart; instead, you are speaking in the dialect of the wounded.
You are letting your soul *exhale.*

For too long, you held it in.
Because no one gave you permission.
Because grief made others uncomfortable.
Because rage didn't fit the version of "you" that people wanted to see.

But here, now, **you have permission.**

Cry if you need to.
Yell if you need to.
Sit in silence if that's all you have.

That's lament too.

You might be angry at God.
You might feel abandoned.
You might wonder where He was when it all happened.

That's okay.
God is not fragile.
He doesn't need you to protect Him from your pain.
He desires truth in the *inmost parts. (Psalm 51:6)*

Lament is how we *witness* our grief before it becomes bitterness.
It's how we bring our ache to the only One who can hold it without flinching.

It's not for show.
It's not performative.
It's intimate.

It's between your soul and your Creator.

There will be days when the pain wells up without warning.
Smells, songs, memories, and moments you thought were behind you.

Let them rise and let them speak.

Suppressing grief doesn't heal it; listening to it does.

You may be afraid that if you open that door, you'll never stop crying. That your sorrow will drown you.

But grief isn't here to destroy you.
It's here to *move through you.*

Like a wave.
Not to crush, but to cleanse.

And God is not on the shore watching.
He's in the water with you.

Lament makes room for your soul to breathe again.
It says:
"I will not carry this alone."
"I will not keep pretending I'm fine."
"I will trust that my tears are safe here."

Because they are.

Part III: Sacred Rage

There's a kind of anger that survivors feel, which no one prepares us for.

It's not a petty irritation.
It's not mood swings.
It's *sacred rage*, the fire that rises when we finally realize what was done to us.

And too often, we're told to quiet it down.

Especially if you're a woman, a Christian, or both, you were likely taught that anger is unbecoming. That rage is sinful.
That to be godly is to be sweet, compliant, and silent.

But Scripture doesn't say that.
God doesn't say that.

Be angry and do not sin.

— (Ephesians 4:26)

Anger itself is not the enemy.
It's a *signal.*
A sacred one.

It tells us: "This was wrong."
"This should never have happened."
"This deserves justice."

Your rage is not a sign you're falling apart.
It's a sign you're *waking up.*

You are no longer suppressing what hurt you.
You are no longer protecting the image of those who harmed you.
You are no longer numbing what God Himself calls evil.

You are calling it what it is.
And your soul is rising up in protest.

There's something holy about that.
Because to feel rage is to recognize that *you matter.*

Your body matters.
Your safety matters.
Your innocence mattered.

And when those things were violated, you had every right to be
angry, even if no one ever told you that.

Jesus turned over tables in the temple.
He cracked whips.
He defended the vulnerable with burning words.

Rage, in the hands of righteousness, is not destructive.
It is *restorative.*

Your anger isn't just about the past.
It's also about the systems that failed you.
The silence of the church.
The complicity of family members.
The way justice still feels out of reach.

That fire inside you isn't just trauma.
It's a divine protest against evil.

But sacred rage has to be *witnessed* to be transformed.

If you deny it, it turns inward.
If you avoid it, it leaks into places it doesn't belong.
But if you bring it into the light, with God, with safe people, with
honesty, it becomes power.
It becomes fuel.
It becomes *fire that warms, rather than burns.*

You don't have to act on every feeling.
You don't have to scream in the face of your abuser.
But you *do* have to let the fire speak.

Through writing.
Through art.
Through movement.
Through prayer.

You are allowed to express your fury in ways that are *honest and safe.*

Your anger is not a curse.
It's a compass.
And when you let God hold it with you,
it becomes a force for healing instead of destruction.

Chapter 14: Learning to Trust Again & Rebuilding Safety Inside and Out

Trusting Yourself And Reclaiming Instinct, Intuition, and Inner Wisdom

"You will keep in perfect peace those whose minds are steadfast, because they trust in You."

— (Isaiah 26:3)

For many survivors, the first betrayal wasn't just what someone did to them, it was what they were told to believe about it.

You were taught to second-guess yourself, to reinterpret abuse as love, and to question your memories, your motives, your *mind*.

You learned to silence the voice inside you that screamed: *"This isn't right."*

Over time, that silencing becomes internal. Once it has taken control over you, then you don't need anyone else to gaslight you.
You start doing it to yourself.

You walk into a room and feel something's off, but you tell yourself you're being dramatic. Or when someone crosses a boundary... and you convince yourself to stay quiet. You feel anxious... and shame yourself for being "too sensitive."

But what if your body isn't lying?
What if your instincts are actually *brilliant?*

"The Spirit Himself bears witness with our spirit..."

— (Romans 8:16)

You have a God-given *inner witness.* It is a sense that says, "Pay attention," and a knowing that doesn't need external approval to be valid.

That's not paranoia, that's survival wisdom, Holy Spirit discernment, and that's trauma-informed *intelligence.*

Trusting yourself again means learning to listen, without judgment. To pause when your body tenses, to get curious when your stomach knots, or to ask: *"What's this sensation trying to tell me?"*

And then to believe that the answer matters.

This doesn't mean you'll always be right, because no one is. But it means you give yourself permission to *try*, trust your perception of the world again, and move from hyper-vigilance to *holy vigilance.*

To say, "I don't need proof to set a boundary. My peace is reason enough.

Part of reclaiming trust in yourself means rejecting the notion that healing must involve total openness.

You don't have to give everyone the benefit of the doubt. You don't have to explain your boundaries. You don't have to keep people in your life who make you feel unsafe, even if they're family. Even if they say, *"But I love you."*

Love without safety is not love, and your intuition knows the difference.

When you begin to trust yourself, you stop asking others for permission to feel what you feel. Then you ultimately stop outsourcing your reality, and you stop minimizing your pain to make others comfortable.

You take up space.
You speak with clarity.
You live with sacred agency.

And the people who are meant to walk with you? They'll recognize that self-trust not as a threat, but as the beginning of your *return to wholeness.*

Reflection Invitation:

- Where in your life are you still operating from survival mode, even though the danger has passed?

- What would it look like to trust that you are safe now, and how might that change the way you show up in the world?

Prompt Reflection Page

Chapter 15: The Healing Toolkit

Part I: Boundaries Are Not Barriers, They Are Bridges to Safety

"Let what you say be simply 'Yes' or 'No'; anything more than this comes from evil."

— Matthew 5:37

Many survivors were never taught that the word *no* was an option. Especially not if it disrupted peace, upset someone they loved, and if the person demanding a *yes* held power.

You were trained to accommodate, remain quiet, and be agreeable.

Because when *no* meant punishment, *yes* became survival.

That's the legacy of trauma: It conditions you to believe that your comfort must always come last.
That your body isn't yours.
That your instincts are rude.
That your refusal is rebellion.

So, when you begin to set boundaries in adulthood, it feels *wrong*.
You feel guilty.
You feel selfish.
You feel afraid that saying *no* will cost you love.

But here's the truth:
Boundaries are not rejection; instead, they are revelations.

They show you who is safe and who only loved you when you were easy to control.

Boundaries are not barriers.
They are bridges.
They allow love to flow *in health.*
They protect what's sacred.
They honor your voice, your space, your worth.

They are not just practical, they are *holy.*

"Above all else, guard your heart, for everything you do flows from it."

— (Proverbs 4:23)

Guarding your heart doesn't mean building walls.
It means creating gates.
It means choosing who gets access, how much, and on what terms.

It means *you* decide what is okay and what is not.

A boundary is not control, it's clarity.

- "I won't stay on the phone if you raise your voice."

- "I'm not available for that conversation right now."

- "I need time to process before I respond."

- "I'm not comfortable being around that person."

You don't have to justify.
You don't have to convince.
You don't have to apologize.

Your boundary is valid because *you exist.*

Jesus had boundaries.
He withdrew from the crowds.
He said no to premature miracles.
He refused to answer manipulative questions.
He walked away from those who only wanted to trap Him.

And if the Son of God could set limits without guilt, so can you.

The people who get angry when you set a boundary are the ones who benefited from your lack of one.

Let that sink in.

Your healing will offend those who relied on your silence, your compliance, your self-abandonment.

But your yes is no longer for their comfort.
It is for your *freedom.*

103

Part II: The Sacred Yes and the Holy No & Reclaiming Power Without Guilt

There is a lie that survivors often carry:
If I say no, I will lose love.

That lie was planted early, when your boundaries were ignored, your cries were silenced, and when your resistance was met with punishment, guilt, or shame.

Over time, your no became dangerous, so you stopped using it.

But here's the truth:
"No" is holy.
It is not rebellion.
It is not bitterness.
It is not ingratitude.

It is a declaration of value.
It says, *"I matter too."*

Your "yes" is sacred too, but only when it is given freely.
Not under pressure, not out of fear, and especially, not because you're trying to earn safety or prove your worth.

A coerced yes is not consent.
A yes that betrays your soul is not love.
A yes born from fear is not godly.

God doesn't manipulate your yes.
He honors your no. Do you know why? Because He gives you a choice, and because real love requires freedom.

> *"Now the Lord is the Spirit, and where the Spirit of the Lord is, there is freedom."*
>
> — *(2 Corinthians 3:17)*

Where freedom lives, trust can grow.
Where pressure rules, trauma hides.

This is why learning to say no without guilt is *a healing* **experience.**
It's not just about keeping others out. It's about maintaining your dignity.

104

Reclaiming your no is how you reclaim power.

It might feel awkward at first, it might even shake your voice, and it might bring pushback.

But every time you say:

- "I'm not okay with that,"
- "That doesn't work for me,"
- "Please don't speak to me that way,"
- "I need some space,"

You are declaring:
"I am worth protecting."

Saying no isn't just a personal act.
It's a spiritual one.
You are aligning yourself with the truth.
You are refusing to abandon yourself again.
You are letting your healed self-speak louder than your scared one.

And when you do say yes, it is powerful; it's not about survival, performance, or appeasing danger. It's your heart choosing what is good and life-giving.

You were made for boundaries.
They are not walls of fear, but the architecture of freedom.

You are allowed to build a life that feels safe, sacred, and sane.

Part III: Boundaries with Family, Faith, and Community.

For many survivors, setting boundaries with strangers is not the most challenging part.

It's setting them with *family*, pastors, and old friends.
With the people who say, "But we're blood," "But we raised you," "But God says to honor your parents."

They use words like "respect" and "forgiveness" as a shield against accountability. They want access without responsibility, and connection without change.

But boundaries don't violate honor; **they protect it.**

God never asked you to dishonor yourself to keep someone else comfortable.

> *"Honor one another above yourselves."*
>
> — *(Romans 12:10)*

Notice it says *"one another."*
Honor is mutual, never one-sided. When someone demands honor but does not give it, they are asking for submission, not a relationship.

You are not dishonoring your mother by saying,
"I won't tolerate you speaking to me like that."

You are not rebelling against your father by deciding,
"I will not let my children be alone with him."

You are not betraying your church by saying, "That spiritual leader is unsafe, and I need distance."

You are honoring the temple of God; *you.*

Because you carry the image of God, and to protect yourself is to protect *His image.*

Religious guilt has a way of cloaking abuse in the guise of virtue.
It teaches that saying "no" to toxic people is unkind... unforgiving... and unchristian.

But Jesus Himself overturned tables.
He called out hypocrisy.
He walked away from those who used Scripture to oppress.

Boundaries are not unholy.
Abuse is.

There will be people who say,
"Family is everything."

However, the truth is that **safety is everything.**

And if someone repeatedly violates your peace, they don't get unlimited access to your life.

You can love someone and still choose to maintain a certain distance. You can forgive someone and still choose no contact. You can hope for reconciliation and still protect your children, your body, your mind.

Setting boundaries with family may bring grief.
You might lose relationships.
You might be misunderstood.

But what you gain is your freedom, peace, and most importantly, *yourself.*

And when you find a community, whether it's a church, a circle, or a therapist's office that celebrates your boundaries, you will breathe more easily.

Because safety doesn't silence you.
It *sees* you.
And says: "Your voice matters here."

Part IV: Living Boundaries & Practicing Them as a Lifestyle

Knowing about boundaries is not the same as living them.
In theory, it sounds empowering.
In practice, it can feel terrifying.

Because boundary-setting is not a one-time conversation.
It's a lifestyle shift. A new way of being in the world, rooted in clarity, not fear.

> *"Let your 'Yes' be yes, and your 'No,' no."*
>
> *— (Matthew 5:37)*

This is not just a moral instruction, it's an *invitation to alignment.*

Your words, values, emotions, and behavior all need to align.

You don't have to say yes and then secretly panic.
You don't have to smile and seethe inside.
You don't have to accommodate what drains you just to avoid tension.

Living with boundaries means telling the truth in real time.
"I'm not available for that."
"I changed my mind."
"That doesn't feel right to me anymore."

It's not cruelty; instead, it's *clarity*, and clarity is kind, even when it's uncomfortable.

At first, practicing boundaries will feel like confrontation.
Because for so long, your silence was mistaken for peace.

But silence is not peace. It is what you feel when your nervous system says, "I'm safe here."

Start small:

- Decline a phone call when you're exhausted.

- End a conversation when someone crosses a line.

- Take space after a triggering family visit.
- Leave the room, the group chat, or the table if your safety is threatened.

Each action is a vote for your well-being.
Each no is a yes to something *greater*.

And when you fail, because we all do, be gentle with yourself.
You're not regressing, you're *learning*, growing new muscles, and you're healing in motion.

Boundary practice may stir up grief.
Some people will walk away.
Some relationships will change.

Let them.

Those who are meant to walk with you in your healed life will not be repelled by your power; they will *rise to meet it.*

Eventually, your boundaries won't feel like armor; they'll feel like peace. A quiet knowing that you don't need to explain your dignity.
That you can live with open hands *and* closed doors.
That you can be kind *and* clear.

You won't need everyone to agree with you.
You'll just need *you* to agree with you.
And that will be enough.

Reflection Invitation:

- Where in your life have you struggled to say no, even when your spirit whispered yes to boundaries?
- What would practicing one new boundary this week look like, and how might it serve your healing?

Prompt Reflection Page

Chapter 16: Trusting Again To Navigate Love, Intimacy, and Friendship After Betrayal

"Love always protects, always trusts, always hopes, always perseveres."

— 1 Corinthians 13:7

Trust is supposed to be the bridge between hearts; unfortunately, for many survivors, it became a trap.

You trusted, and they betrayed you. You opened up, and they used it against you. You let someone in, and they hurt you where it hurts the most.

Thus, your body learned: *Never again.*

Maybe now, even good people feel suspicious, every compliment feels like bait, closeness makes your skin crawl, or maybe you don't know if what you think is love or manipulation.

That's not you being cold or bitter; that's your nervous system doing what it was trained to do: **protect you.**

Trauma confuses our compass; it tells us that love is pain, intimacy is danger, and that vulnerability is exposure; therefore, we as survivors armor up.

We withdraw, forcing us to keep conversations at a surface level, so don't reach out when we're hurting. It leads us to testing people before they can test us, and ultimately, we sabotage anything that feels too good.

But, just like every other human, deep inside, we still crave connection.
To be seen.
To be known.
To be *safe* in someone else's presence.

This ache is not weakness, it's divine.

Because we were made for love and not for the counterfeit kind that demands silence, not the type that takes, and not the kind that leaves you smaller.

But the real kind, the kind that reflects God.
The kind that heals you just by being held.
The kind that says: "You don't have to perform to belong."

> *"There is no fear in love. But perfect love drives out fear…"*
>
> — *(1 John 4:18)*

That's the kind of love you deserve, but you may need to *unlearn* everything that came before it.

Trust is not naïveté; it's not letting everyone back in, nor is it pretending nothing happened.

Trust is about choosing again but wisely, slowly, and bravely. But before you can trust someone else, you must learn to trust *yourself*, gut, boundaries, "no," and your voice when it trembles.

***

You can't trust others until you learn to trust the one person who's never left you, **yourself.**

Trauma disconnects you from your inner knowing. Perhaps you were told that your feelings were wrong, or that you would be punished for speaking up. Maybe they twisted God, guilt, or grace in order to silence your instincts.

So now, even when your body screams, you second-guess yourself, over-explain, and apologize for having boundaries. You ask others to validate decisions you already know are right.

This is the wound before the trust: **I don't believe myself.**

But here's the truth: you *do* know, you always have. The only thing you need to do is practice remembering.

Start here:

- When your stomach knots in a conversation, pause.

- When your chest tightens around someone's energy, listen.

- When you feel the urge to fawn, ask what *you* need.

- When something feels peaceful, even if unfamiliar, follow it.

These are not random feelings.
They are your God-given compass pointing home.

Trusting yourself doesn't mean you won't make mistakes.
It means you believe in your ability to recover.
It means you don't abandon yourself, even when things get messy.

It's the sacred practice of saying: "I may not have all the answers, but I will not betray myself to find them."

Begin rebuilding this trust in small ways:

- Choose what you want to eat without asking someone else first.

- Speak up when something doesn't sit right, even if your voice shakes.

- Let yourself rest without explaining why.

- Say no to something just because you *don't want to.*

Every time you honor your inner wisdom, you rewire the wound that said you couldn't be trusted.

Over time, that quiet, steady voice inside you will grow louder.
And when someone crosses a line, you won't need a thousand reasons to walk away.

You'll know, and that learning will be enough.

Trust in yourself is the foundation. When that's firm, you'll be able to test the waters of connection with others.

Not from desperation, but from discernment. Not to fill a void, but to expand the love already living in you.

***

Trusting again is not about finding someone perfect; instead, it's about learning how to spot the fruit of safety. As people will say the right things, but it's their patterns that tell the truth.

Here's what healthy love looks like:

Respect for Your Boundaries

They don't guilt you for saying no; they don't pressure you into closeness. Instead, they listen when you speak about your limits.

Love does not rush; it honors the *pace of healing.*

Open, Non-defensive Communication

You can bring up hard things without fear of retaliation. They don't gaslight, deflect, or twist your words, and they stay present, even in discomfort.

Love doesn't demand perfection; it builds trust through *repair.*

Emotional Consistency

They are the same person in both public and private settings. They don't disappear after intimacy. They don't flood you one day and ghost you the next.

Love doesn't feel like a roller coaster; it feels like *peace.*

Accountability

They take ownership of their mistakes and don't make excuses. They show you over time that they're safe.

Love doesn't avoid responsibility; it *grows* through it.

Now here are some red flags, especially for survivors whose instincts were once ignored:

- They move *too fast* ("I've never felt this way before" within days)
- They make you doubt your memory or feelings (gaslighting)
- They isolate you from friends, faith, or community
- They joke cruelly about sensitive things
- They punish you emotionally when you set a boundary
- They only apologize to end the argument, not to repair the harm

If any of these symptoms appear, trust your body's signals. You do not owe anyone access to your tenderness just because they want it.

And if you've already let someone in who turned out to be unsafe, that does *not* mean you failed.

It means you *risked*, and every risk teaches you something.

What matters is not perfection, but *returning to yourself* more quickly each time.

Survivors sometimes ask, "How will I know it's real this time?"

Here's a sign: You feel *more like yourself* with them, not less.

They don't demand your shrinking; they celebrate your voice and welcome your full humanity, tears, tremors, laughter, and all.

***

There is a kind of love that doesn't make you earn your place, doesn't disappear when you're messy, and doesn't see your trauma as a burden, but as a map of all the places God will restore.

Whether it comes through a partner, a friend, a mentor, or a faith community, **this kind of love exists.** It may not look like what you've seen before, but when you find it, your nervous system will *feel it.*

Healing love is marked by:

- **Presence without pressure**
- **Listening without fixing**
- **Touch that asks and honors your answer**
- **Joy that doesn't demand your performance**
- **Patience with your pace of rebuilding**

This is what Christ-like connection looks like: Love that protects, doesn't rush, and keeps showing up, and it's not only romantic. Friendship can be profoundly healing.

A friend who sees past your silence. Who texts just to check in? Who sits beside you without trying to solve you? Who reminds you you're lovable even when you're not "productive"?

After betrayal, the idea of *letting someone close* again can feel terrifying. You may brace for loss the moment something good begins. You may withhold parts of yourself, thinking, "If they knew the whole story, they'd leave."

But here's the miracle: Every time you risk being seen and are met with care, your body heals a little more. This is the work of redemption.

Not forgetting the past, but *reclaiming* your ability to love and be loved without fear.

God is not asking you to force trust. He's asking you to *walk with Him* as He reintroduces you to what safe connection feels like.

You were created for intimacy, for deep companionship, and for covenant-level safety. While humans will still be imperfect, God can use relationships to *restore what trauma stole.*

You may not yet know how to open up fully. That's okay, you don't have to rush, and you don't have to push.

You can begin with:

- One honest answer instead of a people-pleasing one
- One safe friend instead of isolation
- One shared tear instead of stuffing it down
- One prayer that says, "God, I want to trust again, help me."

You are allowed to love again.
More than that, you are *worthy* of love that nourishes, protects, and endures.

Reflection Invitation:

- What would trusting again look like for you right now, without pressure or perfection?
- How might God be inviting you to risk connection again, one safe step at a time?

Prompt Reflection Page

Chapter 17: Rewriting the Story to Move From Victimhood to Meaning

"You intended to harm me, but God intended it for good to accomplish what is now being done, the saving of many lives."

— *Genesis 50:20*

There is a holy difference between being a victim and living as one.

You were a victim, and that was a real experience. It was not your fault, and it deserves to be named, but that's not where the story ends.

Staying in victimhood means continuing to define yourself by what was done to you. It keeps you tethered to the pain instead of anchored in purpose.

It says, "I am broken." Instead of, "I was broken... and now I'm rebuilding."

Many survivors struggle here. They either minimize their pain entirely, saying, "I'm fine, it wasn't that bad," or they dwell in it forever, saying, "This is who I am, and I'll never be more."

Both responses are trauma speaking, and both miss the truth: you were harmed, but you are not only your harm.

Rewriting your story isn't about pretending it didn't happen; it's about reclaiming your voice within it.

Instead of: "They destroyed me," you say: "I was devastated... and I rose."

Instead of: "I am damaged," you say: "I carry wounds... and I also carry wisdom."

Your story is allowed to hold both pain and power.
Grief and growth.
Tears and triumph.

Healing is the act of standing inside your own narrative and declaring, "I get to tell it now."

This doesn't mean romanticizing what happened. God never calls evil good, but He does specialize in redemption. He takes the ugliest scenes and writes mercy into the margins. He doesn't erase the scars; instead, he makes them evidence.

Evidence that you lived. That you endured, you're still here, and you're not done becoming.

Letting go of victimhood doesn't mean forgetting what happened. It means *freeing yourself* from being defined by it.

You can acknowledge injustice without staying entangled in it. You can validate your trauma and still move forward with hope.

This chapter is not about rushing your recovery. It's about gently recognizing when the wound has become a wall.

And asking:
"What else is true about me?"
"What meaning might rise from the ashes?"
"What do I want the next chapter to say?"

***

The pain you went through does not become beautiful just because you survived it. But meaning, meaning can make it bearable. Meaning makes the suffering count.

Meaning-making is the spiritual and emotional process of asking: "How has this pain shaped me, and who am I becoming because of it?"

Not: "Why did this happen to me?" But: "What might I do with what has happened?"

Trauma steals clarity; it makes the world feel random and cruel. Meaning gives you back agency.

It doesn't justify what was done, but it allows you to respond with intention.

Meaning can look like:

- Deciding to protect others from the harm you endured

- Becoming an advocate, therapist, writer, or mother who breaks cycles

- Speaking your truth, even if just to yourself

- Reconnecting with God through the very questions that once felt like betrayal

- Choosing softness when the world expects you to be hard

Joseph's words in Genesis 50:20 aren't just theology; they are testimony.

"You intended to harm me, but God intended it for good…"

Not the harm itself, but the good God would bring from it.

Joseph still named the betrayal. He still held the boundary, but he chose meaning over bitterness.
Redemption over revenge.

As a survivor, your testimony isn't just that something bad happened.
It's that you're still here.
That your soul still speaks.
That you're choosing love when hate would be easier.

Sometimes, the meaning arrives slowly.
That's okay.

You don't have to force purpose.
You can simply stay open to it.

Keep walking, healing, and as you do, threads will begin to weave themselves.

One day, your pain may be the very reason someone else finds freedom.

Not because you were sacrificed for them, but because you survived and decided to shine.

That is testimony.

You don't need a platform to change the world.
You just need your truth.

Your healing is holy, and your story, rewritten in your own voice, is a sermon in motion.

***

You are not the only one writing your story; God holds the pen, too.

But He doesn't write over you, and He writes with you. He invites you to co-author a life where trauma doesn't get the final say.

Some people imagine God as distant, an editor who only corrects grammar or punishes plotlines. But the truth is gentler, more stunning: God is a collaborator. A redeemer who takes every torn page and finds a way to make beauty of it.

This doesn't mean that everything happens for a reason. It means that nothing is wasted when placed in God's hands.

Even the broken chapters, the ones you wish you could skip, can become bridges to someone else's healing and your own transformation.

Co-writing with God begins by surrendering the parts you've tried to control through shame.

The lines you've written in fear: "I'll never be loved," "I'm too damaged," and "My life will always feel like this." Let Him help you revise.

Let Him speak back:

"You are loved already."
"You are whole even with wounds."
"There is joy ahead you haven't yet imagined."

When you let God shape the story, you don't erase your pain. You reclaim your hope.

Your faith doesn't deny what happened. It declares that what happens next can be different.

This is not passive. You're still the narrator. Still, the voice in the text.

But now, you're joined by a whisper: "Keep going. I'm writing with you."

Ask Him:

- "What do you want to do with this pain?"
- "What do you see in me that I've forgotten?"
- "Where are you writing redemption? I haven't noticed yet."

Then, listen to the answers; they may not come all at once. But over time, the page will fill.

And when you stand at the edge of a new season, you'll look back on chapters you thought would break you, and realize they built you.

Because God doesn't just restore, He *rewrites.*
Not by removing the truth, but by adding meaning, grace, and a new direction.

> *"And we know that in all things God works for the good of those who love him..."*
>
> — *(Romans 8:28)*

This is the story now: Not just what they did to you, but what *God is doing in you.*

***

Now comes the part no one else can write but you, the next chapter of your life.

Only you can write the script of your life, and you can do so by breaking your silence, healing your trauma that they have tried to engrave in your nervous system. However, that is only possible if you choose to see yourself with clear eyes and a steady heart.

You will have to begin by asking yourself, what kind of life do you want? Not just what you *don't* like, but what you *long for.*

Joy that doesn't scare you, peace that doesn't feel foreign, relationships where you can breathe, mornings that don't begin in dread, and a voice that speaks freely and without apology.

These are not fantasies; they are *your inheritance*, but you have to claim them.

To write a new chapter means choosing, sometimes daily, to walk differently.

It means releasing roles that have kept you small, risking change when comfort says, "Stay," and it means becoming someone who believes they are worth the life they've prayed for.

This will help you choosing a new story isn't always glamorous. Sometimes it's doing the next right thing in quiet faith, and sometimes it's just waking up and *not quitting.*

But every step you take toward wholeness, even the shaky ones, counts as holy ground.

God isn't watching to see if you get it all right.
He's cheering every time you choose life over survival.

So, ask yourself: What story do I want to live from now on?

What do I want my future self to look back on and say: "That's when it turned. That's when I started living like I mattered."

Because you do, you matter, so does your story, and the rest of it is still unwritten.

You are not stuck in the past, as you are *standing on the edge of a future* shaped by wisdom, courage, and mercy.

Reflection Invitation:

- If you could rewrite the next chapter of your life in complete freedom, what would it include?

- What is one small step you can take today to live like that story is already unfolding?

Prompt Reflection Page

Chapter 18: Letters to Survivors, You Are Not Alone

"Even to your old age and gray hairs, I am he, I am he who will sustain you. I have made you and I will carry you; I will sustain you and I will rescue you."

— Isaiah 46:4

To the Survivor Who Has Never Told a Soul

You are not invisible, not to me, and not to God.

The silence you carry is not weakness. It is the sound of survival, and even in the quiet, your pain speaks volumes.

I know it's terrifying to say it out loud, what happened, what it cost you, how long you've held your breath.

But hear me gently: You are allowed to tell the truth, even if your voice shakes, and even if no one else believes it yet.

God saw, and He knows. He calls you *whole*, not because it didn't break you, but because He's still holding the pieces.

To the Survivor Who Feels Ashamed

That shame is not yours to carry.

It was planted by someone else, nurtured by lies, watered by fear, and made to feel like it was your own.

But listen to me closely: You are not dirty, not ruined, and you are not the cause.

You were sinned *against*, and that is not your sin to bear. There is nothing broken in you that disqualifies you from love, belonging, or beauty.

You are sacred, yet you are still chosen, and your worth never leaves you, not for a second.

To the Survivor Still in the Thick of It

I see the way you clutch your breath just to make it to bedtime. I can feel the tremors that no one else notices. I can see the way your body has been holding tension like armor, and the way you pretend to be time just because you are tired of explaining. But remember, this is not the end.

There is a dawn on the other side of this night, there are people waiting to love you in the light, and there is a God who isn't ashamed to sit with you in the dark.

Keep breathing, keep showing up, and you don't have to have it all figured out; instead, you only need to take the next step.

To the Survivor Who Is Healing Out Loud

You are so brave, and it takes courage to speak what others tried to bury. It takes grit to stand in front of your own pain and say, "I will not be quiet anymore."

You don't owe the world your entire story, but the fact that you are choosing to share it, even with just one trusted soul, is an act of rebellion against shame.

Your voice is not too much, your pain is not too messy, and your truth is *holy ground.*

And every time you name what happened, you give someone else permission to heal. Therefore, keep going, and your honesty is a lighthouse.

To the Survivor Who Is Still Angry

Your anger makes sense, of course.

Anger is what happens when your body remembers an injustice that your voice wasn't safe enough to express.

It's what rises when the world tries to move on before you've even had a chance to process. God is not afraid of your anger. He doesn't shame you for feeling what's real.

In fact, righteous anger can be part of healing, part of reclaiming your agency, your worth, and your right to justice.

Let it move through you, and don't suppress it. But don't let it become your home either.

Let anger lead you to grief, let grief lead you to healing, and let healing lead you to peace, the kind that honors the truth but doesn't stay stuck in the storm.

To the Survivor Who Wonders If It's Too Late

It is not too late, not to speak, not to grieve, and not to begin again.

Whether you are 17 or 70, your story is still breathing. There is no expiration date on restoration.

You may feel like you've missed your chance, as if too much time has passed, and that healing belongs to younger people with more years ahead of them.

But healing is not about time; it's about *truth.*

And it is never too late to step into the truth and find that it holds you, gently, entirely, without judgment.

You are not behind; you are exactly where your heart is ready to begin.

To the Survivor Who Doesn't Believe in God

I understand why you don't. When the people who were supposed to protect you didn't, when the prayers went unanswered, when silence echoed louder than mercy, it makes sense that you questioned it all.

You don't have to pretend. You don't have to force belief just to make someone else comfortable. What happened to you was real, and if you're angry with God, you're allowed to say so.

He can handle it. He doesn't withdraw in the face of your pain. He moves toward it.

Whether or not you believe in Him, He believes in *you.*

He knows the full weight of what you've carried, and He has never stopped seeing you as worthy of love.

If you ever find yourself whispering into the dark, know this: God hears even the questions that come with clenched fists, and He's still near.

To the Survivor Rebuilding Their Faith

It's okay to rebuild slowly. Maybe you're picking up pieces that once felt sacred, only to realize some were used as weapons. Perhaps you're afraid of being hurt again by people who claim to speak for God.

Faith doesn't mean going back to what broke you. It means *relearning trust* from a God who never harmed you in the first place.

You don't have to rush; You can ask your questions, wrestle with Scripture, light candles in the dark, and ask God to meet you there. He will, He always does.

To the Survivor Who Is Finally Free

You made it through it all. After all the nights you didn't think you would, the memories that clawed at your hope, and all the silent battles no one saw but heaven.

You're still here, and that is a miracle. Freedom doesn't mean nothing hurts anymore; it means you've stopped living in the grip of what happened.

It means you laugh again, you rest again, and you trust again, maybe slowly, maybe differently,
but beautifully.

You are not who they said you were; you never were.

You are beloved, resilient, and whole.

And this? This is just the beginning.

Reflection Invitation:

- Which letter resonated most deeply with your current season of healing?

- Write a letter of your own, to your past self, to God, or to another survivor who needs the same reminder you did.

Prompt Reflection Page

Chapter 19: The Healing Practice to Anchor Safety

PART I: Grounding and Returning to the Present

"He will cover you with his feathers, and under his wings you will find refuge; his faithfulness will be your shield and rampart."

— Psalm 91:4

Trauma doesn't just live in memory; instead, it lives in the body. It lingers in your nervous system, manifesting as a racing heart, a tight chest, and hypervigilant thoughts. That's why healing requires more than just talking. It also involves *anchoring,* finding steady ground when your inner world begins to spin out of control. That's where grounding comes in.

Grounding Techniques

Grounding is the practice of returning to the *present moment* when you feel overwhelmed by fear, flashbacks, or dissociation. It tells your body: "I am safe right now."

Here are a few survivor-tested practices to try:

1. 5-4-3-2-1 Sensory Scan

Use your five senses to return to the present:

- 5 things you can see
- 4 things you can touch
- 3 things you can hear
- 2 things you can smell
- 1 thing you can taste

Say each one aloud.
Name the color, describe the texture, and feel it in your mouth. This helps your brain locate safety in the physical world.

2. The Name Game

Pick a category (cities, plants, foods, colors) and name something for every letter of the alphabet. It sounds simple, but it works. This engages your logical brain, which calms your survival brain.

3. Temperature Reset

Run cold water over your hands or face, hold an ice cube, or step outside into the fresh air. Sudden temperature changes can shock your system out of panic and into a state of presence.

4. Anchor Object

Keep a small, meaningful item in your pocket or bag, a cross, a smooth stone, a shell from a beach where you felt safe. Whenever you feel lost, hold it in your hand. Let it remind you: I am here. I am okay. I am not alone.

5. Breathwork for Safety

When panic rises, breath can become shallow. Instead, try this rhythm:

- Inhale for 4 seconds
- Hold for 4 seconds
- Exhale for 6 seconds
- Repeat for 2–3 minutes

As you exhale, say to yourself, "I am safe. I am loved. I am held."

You can even picture yourself being sheltered under God's wing, like the verse says. Covered. Protected. These practices are not just coping mechanisms; they are *tools for reconnection*.

They remind you that you have a body. That your body has wisdom. And that you are allowed to feel grounded again.

PART II: Listening to the Body — Somatic Awareness, Boundaries, and Inner Child Work

Your body remembers. Even when your mind forgets or tries to minimize what happened, your body holds the truth. That's why trauma healing must include a return to your physical self, not to relive the pain, but to reclaim *ownership*.

Somatic Awareness

Somatic healing is the practice of noticing your body's cues and responding with compassion.

You can start with small daily check-ins:

- Where in my body do I feel tension today?

- What emotion lives in that part?

- What would help it soften?

Maybe it's your shoulders gripping old fear, your jaw holds unshed words, and your stomach flutters with unspoken dread.

Place your hand there, and breathe into it, then whisper, "You're allowed to let go now."

Boundaries: Physical and Emotional

Boundaries are not walls. They are *doors with locks*. You get to choose who comes in, how far they can go, and when. Trauma often teaches us that we don't have that right, but part of recovery is remembering:

Your body is yours.
Your space is sacred.
Your no is holy.

Start by practicing with small things:
"I don't want to hug right now."
"I need time to think before I respond."
"I'm not comfortable discussing that topic."

Each boundary you set teaches your nervous system: *We are safe now. We are in control.*

Inner Child Work

Every survivor has a younger version of themselves still inside. The child who was scared, who froze, and who didn't get to finish crying. Inner child work is about reparenting, offering that little one what they never received.

You might:

- Write a letter to your child self
- Place your hand over your heart and whisper, "You did nothing wrong."
- Imagine holding her. Rocking her. Telling her she's safe now
- Let her speak. Let her draw. Let her rest

This is not regression, it's *repair.*

God doesn't just heal your adult self. He loves the child you were, too.

The child who survived, and the child didn't deserve what happened to them. When you nurture that part of you, you participate in the divine act of restoration. You don't have to be fully healed to start this work. You just need to be present, and every time you pause to listen to your body, you honor its role in your survival. And now? You teach it how to feel safe in love again.

PART III: Mental Reframes To Naming Lies, Speaking Truth, and Rewriting Thought Patterns

Trauma doesn't just bruise the body; it rewires the mind. Thoughts once formed in fear can become the default settings of our inner dialogue. Over time, those thoughts feel like the truth. But they're often just *survival scripts* written by pain.

Reframing is the act of interrupting those scripts. Of pausing and asking, "Is this thought true? Or is this the trauma talking?" It's not about toxic positivity. It's about reclaiming your mental landscape—thought by thought, truth by truth.

Common Trauma-Induced Lies:

1. **"It was my fault."**
   → Reframe: *"What happened was not okay, and it was never my fault. The blame belongs to the one who caused harm."*

2. **"I'm too broken to be loved."**
   → Reframe: *"I am healing, not broken. Love isn't a reward for perfection—it's a birthright."*

3. **"I should be over this by now."**
   → Reframe: *"Healing takes time, and I am exactly where I need to be."*

4. **"I'll never be safe again."**
   → Reframe: *"I am building a life where safety is possible. And I'm allowed to feel safe now."*

5. **"No one will ever understand me."**
   → Reframe: *"There are people out there who can hold space for my story. I don't have to do this alone."*

Practice: Catch, Challenge, Change

Catch the thought: "I'm a burden."

Challenge it: Where did this belief come from? Would I say this to a friend who went through what I did?

Change it: "I am worthy of care. My needs matter. I am loved even when I need help."

You don't have to *believe* the new thought right away; you just need to start speaking it. Eventually, your brain will follow your voice.

Spiritual Reframing

God never said you're unworthy. He never called you dirty, ruined, or irredeemable. Those voices may have come from abusers, culture, or even twisted versions of religion, but *not from Him.*

Scripture says you are:

- **"Fearfully and wonderfully made" (Psalm 139:14)**
- **"More than a conqueror" (Romans 8:37)**
- **"A new creation" (2 Corinthians 5:17)**
- **"Chosen, holy, and dearly loved" (Colossians 3:12)**

Let these truths be your mental anchors. When shame speaks, speak back with scripture. You are not a problem to fix. You are a person to love.

PART IV: Sacred Practices for Faith-Based Anchors and Daily Rituals for Healing

Faith is not a shortcut through pain; it's a shelter within it.

For many survivors, trauma and faith coexist in complicated tension. However, some were hurt *in* church, while others questioned God in the aftermath. Still others clung to Him when nothing else made sense.

Wherever you are on your spiritual path, there is room for sacred ritual. Room to reconnect, rebuild, and rest in something bigger than yourself.

Scripture Meditation

Instead of reading large chunks, choose one short verse.
Sit with it, and let it breathe.

Example:

"The Lord is close to the brokenhearted."

— Psalm 34:18

Breathe in: *"The Lord is close…"*
Breathe out: *"…to the brokenhearted."*

Let the words wrap around your nervous system like a warm blanket, and repeat them until they start to feel true.

Candlelight Prayer

Set aside five quiet minutes, then light a candle, and let its flame remind you of God's constant presence.

Speak aloud or in silence:

- "God, I'm tired."
- "God, I'm still here."
- "God, help me hold what I can't carry alone."

You don't need fancy words, as God understands groans, whispers, and even silence.

Prayer Journaling

Pour your heart onto the page as if writing to a trusted friend.

You can start with prompts like:

- "God, this is what hurts today…"
- "God, where were You when…?"
- "God, thank You for…"

Write without censoring and let your journal be a sanctuary for truth.

Embodied Prayer

Prayer isn't just spoken.
It can be embodied.

- Kneel when you feel small and want to be covered
- Stretch your arms wide when you need freedom
- Place a hand over your heart when asking for comfort
- Lay prostrate when surrendering to pain

Your body is not a distraction from prayer; it can *become* the prayer.

Daily Rituals of Hope

Healing happens in the ordinary.
It's the tiny daily habits that become anchors over time.

Try any of the following:

- Begin your morning with one breath of gratitude
- End your night by listing 3 moments of grace
- Keep a "Truth Box" with handwritten scriptures to pull when overwhelmed
- Create a sacred playlist of worship songs that soothe your soul
- Take a short walk and name what you see as a moving meditation

Each small act says, "I am alive. I am worthy of peace. I am loved."

These sacred practices don't make the pain disappear, but they remind you of who walks with you through it.

God never promised an easy life, but He did promise His nearness, His comfort, His rescue, and His Word never fails.

PART V: Support Systems to Build Safe Circles, Therapeutic Help, and Spiritual Community

Healing is not meant to be done alone. Though trauma may have isolated you, recovery invites you back into connection, safe, chosen, intentional connection.

Whether through a therapist's office, a trusted friend, or a faith-filled support group, community can become holy ground.

Building Safe Circles

Not everyone deserves full access to your story, but *someone* should be allowed to carry it with you.

A safe person is someone who:

- Listens without trying to fix
- Doesn't flinch at your truth
- Honors your boundaries
- Doesn't use your vulnerability against you
- Walks with you instead of ahead of you

You don't need a crowd, you just need consistency.

Start with one. Let trust grow slowly, like a tender vine, not forced, just fed.

Therapeutic Support

Trauma-informed therapy can be life-changing. Whether it's CBT (Cognitive Behavioral Therapy), EMDR (Eye Movement Desensitization and Reprocessing), or somatic therapy, these approaches are crafted to address trauma at its roots.

A good therapist:

- Believes your story
- Honors your pace
- Helps rewire trauma responses
- Offers practical tools for daily life

138

If finances are tight, search for:

- Sliding scale clinics
- Faith-based counseling centers
- Nonprofit mental health organizations
- Online platforms offering reduced rates

You are not weak for needing help; you are wise for seeking it.

Spiritual Community That Heals

Not every church is trauma-safe, but the body of Christ is meant to be a refuge, not a battlefield.

Look for communities that:

- Preach grace over guilt
- Believe survivors
- Empower women and protect children
- Offer support groups or counseling
- Understand the role of mental health in spiritual healing

You are allowed to leave churches that harm you, and you are allowed to find new spiritual homes that nourish you. The Church is more than a building; it's the people who see you, stay with you, and lead you closer to Jesus.

Ask for What You Need

One of the most challenging steps in the healing process is *reaching out.*

Say:

- "Can I tell you something hard?"
- "I don't need fixing. I just want to be heard."
- "Would you pray with me?"
- "Can we talk, even if I cry?"

You don't have to be eloquent, you just have to be honest.

The right people will hold your truth gently.

God often heals through people, through hugs that last longer than pain, conversations that don't end in judgment, and the presence of quiet, steady, and sacred moments. You don't have to be healed to be held.

Reflection Invitation:

- Who in your life feels safe enough to walk with you in healing?
- If no one comes to mind, what qualities would a safe person need to have, and what is one small step you can take to seek that connection?

Prompt Reflection Page

Epilogue: You Are the Evidence

"They overcame him by the blood of the Lamb and by the word of their testimony."

— *Revelation 12:11a*

You made it! You have made it through every jagged chapter, through the silence that tried to swallow you, through the ache of remembering and the trembling of telling the truth, you came through, and you didn't just survive; you *transformed.*

The world may never fully grasp the weight of what you've carried, but heaven has recorded every sigh, every tear, every brave whisper that said, "I want more than just survival."

You are not broken beyond repair, nor are you evidence of resurrection.

Your scars tell the story, not just of what was done to you, but of what couldn't kill your spirit.
What couldn't erase your worth? What couldn't stop the sacred within you from rising?

Your story doesn't end with the abuse, it doesn't end with fear, nor does it end with healing.

It continues in the way you love now, in the way you notice others in pain, or the way your voice breaks the silence for those still locked in shame.

You are a mirror of hope and a lighthouse for others finding their way.

To speak your truth is to unravel darkness, and to heal out loud is to rewrite generational stories with your bare hands and your beating heart.

You don't owe anyone a tidy ending. Healing is not a final destination; it is a rhythm. A series of sacred choices made over and over again: To get back up, rest, believe, and bless yourself with gentleness even when the world doesn't understand. If ever you forget who you are, come back here.

Read these words again: You are not ruined, you are not to blame, you are not too late, and you are not alone. You are the evidence that survival is possible, and restoration is real. You are the evidence that God is still in the business of bringing beauty from ashes.

Let the world see you, let them hear you, and let them witness what healing looks like in real time. You are living proof that the past does not get the final word. You are the evidence, and evidence changes everything.

www.ingramcontent.com/pod product compliance
Lightning Source LLC
Chambersburg PA
CBHW051528120626
46551CB00012B/1124